Contents

Your Brain at Work

A New View of Personality and Behavior

Dr. Margaret A. Golton

FRANK PUBLICATIONS   New York

QUESTION: Do you think you can change the
world all by yourself?

ANSWER: Individuals have been known to make
a difference. I would like to try.

Library of Congress Cataloging in Publication Data.

Golton, Margaret A.
    Your brain at work.

    Biliography: p. 113
    1. Personality. 2. Brain. I. Title.
BF698.G565   1983   155.2   83-14176

ISBN 0-942952-01-4

Published by
Frank Publications
60 East 42nd St.
Suite 757
New York, N.Y. 10017

Acknowledgments

Gratitude beyond bounds goes to the scientists and theorists who have charted the topography of the brain and made their findings available to all who are interested. I am also grateful from the depths of my being to the individuals who enliven these pages. They listened carefully and respectfully as the BONN theory evolved. They put the procedures to test and generously shared their experiences. They have been pioneers with me in clearing rough, untrod terrain.

To my special coterie of friends, ages thirteen to ninety, my profound thanks:

Those who were on constant alert for the new information on the brain.

Those whose attention I commandeered when excitement broke bounds.

Those who listened with cautious skepticism when my uncautious mind took giant leaps into expanding horizons: They did not know. They could not assess.

They only could listen. This they did patiently.

Implicit in the involvement of all of them has been subtle faith that if what I had undertaken to do could be done, I would do it. Their confidence was sustaining. They enticed me into social involvement. They ensured that my cultural diet was varied and rich. I have been fortunate indeed to have had them on the scene.

Finally, to the team responsible for bringing the manuscript to a finished book: Bonita Vargo for her graphic presentation of the BONN concept; Françoise Bartlett for her generous evaluation of and her dedication in editing the manuscript; Robert Kopelman for the creativity he brought to the design of the cover and the text; and Ben G. Frank for his unwavering confidence and encouragement. Responsibility for the content of these pages is mine alone. I feel privileged to have made the BONN discovery. I feel under great urgency to make it known.

Preface

From Dag Hammerskjold's *Markings*, a legacy:

> He broke new ground because and only because he had the courage to go ahead without asking whether others were following or even understood.

So buttressed, I venture an uncharted course. My search is simple: How can human beings become better equipped to make the most of the amazing world that is unfolding in our lifetime?

Four hundred years ago men were burned at the stake because they believed the world was round. In 1939, scientists were criticized for projecting travel to the moon. In 1959, scientists said the key to life would never be found. Four years later, an English scientist at the University of Cambridge discovered DNA, the building block of human genes.

Resistance to change and especially resistance to new knowledge that requires change is easily understood when one realizes that the human being, like all other natural phenomena, is subject to the three basic laws of nature:

The law of gravity or inertia.
The law of conservation.
The law of magnetism.

Interestingly, in the extensive literature that has accumulated in the last hundred years on the human personality there is no mention of these basic laws as they manifest themselves in the human being. Perhaps we humans have considered ourselves above and beyond the rules that govern other natural things. Egotism may be the word for this; perhaps we feel a sense of superiority to all else. On the other hand, perhaps human mentality has not yet developed to a sufficient level of sophistication to be able to view its own species in relation to the natural world of which it is a part.

Two hundred years ago, according to some scientists, we knew everything there was to know. Today, with the known one thousand times more than it was in 1900, we know nothing about anything. The era of uncertainty was ushered in five hundred years ago with the birth of science. Each new discovery opens the way to new possibilities. Each possibility places in jeopardy what has been accepted as established.

The BONN (Brain Organization/Neural Network) approach to personality and behavior places those concerned with personality development and mental health in much the same position as scientists when the laser was discovered. That it had enormous potential was sensed. How to put that potential into practice remained a puzzle for many years. To the psyche the "how" was equivalent to the effect of an earthquake in nature—an upheaval in psychological terms. Scientists had to set aside Newtonian theory, which had been the basis of their thinking for three hundred years. They had to develop a new theory based on Einstein's discoveries in electromagnetics, a theory rooted in the concept of process rather than product, in unpredictability rather than cause and effect. New perceptions—energy flow, waves, circuitry—emerged. The laser within this context proved an instrument of vast potential. It can fuse steel. It can also be used to effect delicate eye surgery.

To view the human personality in terms of brain research findings that have been uncovered since the 1950s requires a similar recasting. The potentials may be just as great where human beings and the life experience are concerned.

University Heights, Ohio   M.A.G.
May 1983

Introduction

Based on the findings of current brain research, the BONN (Brain Organization/Neural Network) approach postulates:

Personality and behavior stem from brain organization and design preset by nature as are our fingerprints, body structure, and facial features. The organization and design may be similar to that of parents or ancestors. It may be a design previously known to the species. Or it may be an invention consistent with nature's constant striving for improvement, the mutant, the "sport" so common in nature. *THE PRESET BRAIN ORGANIZATION AND DESIGN ARE ALTERABLE BY MEANS OF VERBAL COMMUNICATION ALONE.*

The BONN approach is rooted in a body of knowledge. It is based on a theory of personality that encompasses the developmental and the dynamic. It employs specific, identifiable procedures and offers guidelines for assessing change and mastery.

The distinguishing feature of the BONN theory and practice is its lack of concern for history, personal or family. Life experience is considered for clues to mastery, for clues to the developmental level that has been achieved as it relates to the individual's potential. Attention is focused on two issues:

Which section of the brain is in control—the limbic section (emotions), the right hemisphere (imagination, fantasy), or the left hemisphere (knowledge, logic, reason, and judgment, with a keen sense of reality and time)?

Is the neural network design complex or simple, with many points of connection or few, with one or more centers of control through which stimuli flow? Are there loops, short circuits, dead ends, and loose ends in the neural network design? All of this to be determined by verbal communication alone.

Your Brain at Work provides indicators for determining whether the individual has a firmly developed self or one that is uncentered, possibly even undifferentiated. It provides procedures for changing brain organization and design so that the three sections of the brain operate in harmony, consistent with the individual's values, priorities, and goals. All of this is to be accomplished by verbal interaction alone.

The BONN approach examines only two aspects of the brain: (1) its organization—which of the three sections of the brain is in control? and (2) neural network design and adequacy—are there sufficient neural channels for the different sections of the brain to be in communication and are there irregularities in the design of the neural network—loops, short circuits, dead ends, and loose ends that interfere with appropriate functioning? In this examination we must keep in mind:

The evolutionary history of each section.

The specific, unique characteristics of each section.

The adequacy of the governing unit, the executive "I" or the personucleus.

The bias of the book is specific. If nature had intended the human species to survive on the basis of instinct, reflex, and habit (the operational patterns of the limbic section and right hemisphere), it would not have doubled the size of the brain 300,000 years ago and created the left hemisphere with its specific attributes: ability to acquire knowledge, exercise logic, reason, and judgment, and keenly perceive reality and time. It is by virtue of its existence that the left hemisphere has authority rather than by virtue of its evolutionary seniority.

A theory, much like the human organism, is not born full blown. It emerges step by step, thought by thought, idea by idea. Sometimes the progress is upward, pyramidal, from broad base to pinnacle. Sometimes it is downward, from pinnacle to broad base. The mind investigates, sorts out, and pieces together in its search for the underlying elements that fuse and coagulate the theory. We proceed from knowledge to action and from action to knowledge. The venture is an exciting one, enticing the mind ever onward as completely unanticipated questions break into consciousness.

When my marriage of forty-three and a half years came to an abrupt end without prior warning at the decree of nature, I had no idea that my determination to survive would lead me to a breakthrough in personality theory: *The Promise of the Womb: A Hoax.* Nor was there any way I could have foreseen that that breakthrough would lead me into brain research and to what I believe is a major discovery—the source of human personality and behavior.

I know full well what an immodest claim this is. I know with equal certainty the significance of my discovery. The discovery carries with it a mandate to make my findings known. My book *Unlock Your Potential: Know Your Brain and How It Works* makes available to everyone my experiences and conclusions with two groups of people: those who would like their lives to be better (the quality seekers) and those who want their lives to be different (the innovators). Dr. James Plant pointed out many years ago that we learn from people with problems what every individual struggles with. It was his theory that guided my writing.

The present book has a different focus. It deals with problems people experience in relation to themselves, to others, and to situations. It is addressed to parents, educators, clinicians, mentors, and self-developers. How to keep the archaic sections of the brain from interfering with left hemisphere activity is its thrust.

The theory on which this book is based has been in germination since approximately 1975. The procedures have been in operation since November 1978. Approximately 200 individuals ranging in age from 10 to 83 years (median, 35–45) and equally divided between men and women have been involved. The problems have been equally wide in range: smoking, obesity, learning problems, difficulties in relationships, sexual compulsion, and borderline and blatant psychoses. The procedures are simple; the results, dramatic. Achievements generalize from the specific problem to life management as a whole.

As we consider the brain with its multidimensional characteristics we can understand the dilemma of the six blind men trying to arrive at a comprehensive view of the elephant. Each had experienced one part. Each extrapolated to the whole. To the one who touched the tusk, the elephant was a spear. To the one who touched the side, the elephant was a wall. The leg carried the image of a tree; the trunk, a snake; the ear, a fan; the tail, a rope. Each was partly right. They were all wrong.

A similar dilemma faces those who would arrive at a comprehensive view of the human personality in all of its multiple, varied dimensions. There may be in the findings of brain research the scheme, the pattern into which each part may fit, yielding a comprehensive view of the whole. Once the underlying scheme becomes clear methods for intervention are likely to prove simple and all-inclusive, much like that piercing beam of light, the laser, that can fuse steel and perform delicate eye surgery. I believe there is in the BONN approach the possibility of such a scheme.

More than forty years of clinical experience are encompassed in these pages. A broad spectrum of human distress is its backdrop: the economic upheaval of the thirties, the wars of the forties, the disparagement of the fifties and the sixties, family dislocations reflected in the needs of dependent children and in the needs of emotionally disturbed children. I have witnessed the development of many different kinds of therapies: gestalt, transactional analysis, the primal scream, biofeedback. I have seen the ebb and flow of eastern philosophy and the cults. Individuals continue to seek a viable, tenable, tolerable way of life. And the search goes on.

PART I

BRAIN ORGANIZATION and DESIGN

CHAPTER 1

The Brain: An Organizational Profile

The brain in its simplest dimension is like an apartment complex, a unit of separate but connected parts. The parts—the limbic section and the right and left hemispheres—came into existence at different points in evolutionary history. Each has unique characteristics and its own source of energy and patterns of energy deployment. Each part also has its own method of responding to stimuli. Some theorists postulate that each part of the brain may have its own level of intelligence.

Connecting the different sections of the brain is a tubelike structure of neural fibers known as the corpus collasum. Decision making occurs in the neural sheath, a narrow band of neural fibers that blankets the top of the right and left hemispheres. Somewhere in the brain is the core, what one might call the "personucleus." Lee Morton Hunt calls this core the "homunculus." It is in the brain but not of the brain. Philosophers over the centuries have called this aspect of the human personality the soul. The personucleus transcends the brain and is of tremendous importance to brain functioning. It is the "boss," the executive "I." It establishes the values, priorities, and goals that give direction to the individual's life.

Sectional Diversity

The Limbic Area

The limbic area of the brain, three million years old, ranks highest in evolutionary seniority. It is the locus of the three autonomic systems without which there cannot be life: respiration, circulation, and appetite. Because of its primacy we may assume that deeply imprinted in its cells is the womb experience. We may assume also that it houses the three basic laws of nature—the law of gravity or inertia, the law of conservation, and the law of magnetism. These laws operate to one degree or another in each individual. Dominance by one rather than another is reflected in what we consider basic personality characteristics. The individual who is dominated by the law of gravity or inertia is likely to prefer the "as is," the status quo. The individual dominated by the law of conservation is likely to be tradition bound, to prefer things as they have been. Where the law of magnetism dominates, the individual is likely to be adventurous, curious, and impatient with the "as is." The limbic area is the locus of primary emotions— love, hate, anger, aggression, passion. Here raw emotions are upgraded into sympathy, empathy, compassion, commitment, dedication.

Because it evolved first and is essential to life itself, the limbic area has vested in it tremendous responsibility. It carries responsibility for reproduction of the species through its sexual attributes. It carries responsibilities for relationships to which it brings all of its emotional capabilities, raw and upgraded. It also carries responsibilities for the individual's sense of awareness and the development of the self-other constellation, a function central to the effective operation of the organism as a whole.

We know that the limbic area is important, yet we know little about it. Thanks to psychoanalysis, we know much more about its evolutionary peer, the right hemisphere. Our lack of knowledge about the limbic area may well be due to the fact that, according to current brain research findings, there are in most brains few, if any, neural connections between the limbic area and the left hemisphere, where knowledge is accumulated. In other words, the limbic area may not have been available for exploration because of the inadequacy of neural connections. Being unavailable for exploration has not made it inoperative, however. The knowledge we have accumulated has left the limbic area untouched. It has remained free to use its tremendous power unfettered, unaffected by the restraints of knowledge, logic, reason, and judgment, the faculties of the left hemisphere. It has been free to function autocratically, as mandated by instinct, reflex, and habit, with no concern for time or reality. Unless it is brought into the domain in which the left hemisphere operates, the limbic area knows only one response: "I want."

The Right Hemisphere:

The right hemisphere is second in evolutionary seniority, some 500,000 years the limbic section's junior. The right hemisphere is the source of imagination, fantasy, daydreaming, and wishing. It can sing but cannot speak. It can write poetry but cannot rhyme. The right hemisphere sees things as a whole and has difficulty distinguishing the parts of which the whole is made. Embedded in the cells of the right hemisphere are ancestral memory and species history. There remain traces of the "shoulds," "oughts," and "musts" decreed by ancient "gods." Also present are the "shoulds," "oughts," and "musts" imparted by parents, teachers, and religious training.

The right hemisphere, like the limbic area, has no sense of time. It can juxtapose what happened at birth and what happened a second ago. With no sense of reality, the right hemisphere creates its own reality. It does not concern itself with whether that reality is valid, appropriate, or pertinent to the individual's best interest.

The Left Hemisphere

The left hemisphere is the most recent addition to the brain complex. In order to function properly it has certain requirements. It must have knowledge. Perhaps it does not have at its command the wisdom that has accumulated through the ages from species

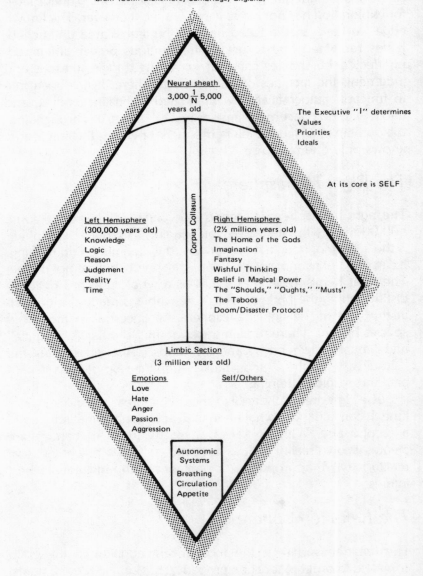

The Executor carries out the orders of the Executive
"I," which is in the brain but not of the
brain (Colin Blakemore, Cambridge, England)

Neural sheath
3,000 $\frac{1}{N}$ 5,000
years old

The Executive "I" determines
Values
Priorities
Ideals

At its core is SELF

Corpus Collasum

Left Hemisphere
(300,000 years old)
Knowledge
Logic
Reason
Judgement
Reality
Time

Right Hemisphere
(2½ million years old)
The Home of the Gods
Imagination
Fantasy
Wishful Thinking
Belief in Magical Power
The "Shoulds," "Oughts," "Musts"
The Taboos
Doom/Disaster Protocol

Limbic Section
(3 million years old)

Emotions   Self/Others
Love
Hate
Anger
Passion
Aggression

Autonomic
Systems

Breathing
Circulation
Appetite

(THE AUTHOR'S VIEW OF BRAIN ORGANIZATION.)

experience and ancestral memory, as do the other sections. Perhaps, unlike the limbic section, it does not have deeply imprinted in its cells the intrauterine experience and so does not have womb-experience expectations. Guided by knowledge, logic, reason, judgment, and reality, the left hemisphere knows that two people do not make one, that wants and needs are not automatically satisfied, that safety and security are not assured once one has left the womb. These possibilities—that the left hemisphere does not have at its command inherited wisdom and that its cells do not carry the imprint of the womb experience—warrant exploration now that we have the instruments with which to explore the contents and behavior of brain cells.

Since the requirements for left hemisphere functioning are outside the experience and capability of the limbic section and the right hemisphere, it is little wonder that the latter protest. It is little wonder that the limbic section and the right hemisphere pull rank, for their authority and power are in jeopardy. What right does this young upstart left hemisphere have to interfere with their traditional way of functioning, with their indisputable evolutionary seniority and the energy they have to assert their power? Why should they heed the left hemisphere? "Why" is a valid question. The answer is equally valid and urgent: because nature so ordered.

The left hemisphere does not operate on inherited knowledge and wisdom. It is keenly aware of objective reality and is extremely sensitive to time—past, present, and future. The left hemisphere thinks, reflects, evaluates, and makes judgments. It observes, compares, and contrasts. It makes connections, sometimes between things that are the same and sometimes between different things. The left hemisphere is inquisitive—it wants to know "why"—and is curious—if this is so, then what? The left hemisphere is inventive: if this works maybe something else will work also. When it is functioning properly it knows its limits. It knows when the knowledge and skills it has are adequate to what it wants to do and when they are not. The left hemisphere has no illusions; no thought of magical power. It knows wishing will not make something happen. It knows if one wants things to happen, one must make them happen.

The Neural Sheath

The neural sheath is a thin band of fibers that strung end to end would reach the planet Saturn.[1] It blankets the top of the left and right hemispheres. It sifts, sorts, and distributes stimuli. These functions Freud ascribed to the ego. We do not know when the neural sheath first appeared in the human brain. It would be a significant coincidence should we find that the appearance of the neural sheath and the development of consciousness occurred at the same time, some three to five thousand years ago, as estimated by psychologist Julian Jaynes.

In current brain organization the neural sheath is the executive branch. It carries out administrative tasks delegated to it by the executive "I," the personucleus.

The Executive "I"

Colin Blakemore, a psychobiologist at the University of Cambridge, England, and active in national and international brain research organizations, has placed the "I," the "me-ness of me," two inches behind the eye in the middle of the brain. That is precisely the location of the pear-shaped pineal gland which processes chemical and electrical stimuli and sends nerveimpulses to the neurological system.[2] Is the "I" located in the pineal gland? Perhaps one day researchers will have established its precise locus. We could then explore the possibility that an impaired self-image or an inadequately developed sense of self may have its roots in the nature, structure, and functioning of the pineal gland. There is a good chance that the "I" has a specific location, that it is more than an amorphous, vacuous figment of someone's imagination. If the "I" has a specific locus, perhaps it will be the subject of serious investigation that will shed light on more effective means of treating persons whose sense of self is impaired.

Where the personality is concerned the "I" is the final authority. In clinical practice one finds over and over again that although its authority is final, it is not absolute. The archaic sections of the brain, the limbic area and the right hemisphere, do not have to accede to the authority of the "I." They can and often do revolt. When the limbic and right hemispheres act in unison against the left hemisphere they exercise formidable power.

The effectiveness of the executive "I" as the final authority depends upon the extent to which separateness in its many dimensions has been achieved. Separateness is a composite of four essential components: autonomy, authenticity, accessibility (to individuals, to community, to cosmos), and actualization. They form the foundation of the self that is whole, firm, and inner directed while related to the outer whole (reality). They provide the psychological substance from which emanate values, priorities, goals—the mainstream of the individual's life experience. The centrality of the "self" will be examined in Part II.

Organization and Pattern Variations

Organization

Brains come in different organizational patterns. In some individuals the limbic section is central. These individuals experience life at "gut" level. Feelings are dominant. In others the right hemisphere dominates. These are the dreamers whose goals often exceed their capabilities. In still other persons the left hemisphere is dominant. They are realistic and practical. Reason, logic, and judgment are in control. Such individuals are often dismissed as "intellectual," unfeeling, and unimaginative.

For maximum effectiveness the three sections of the brain need to work in harmony. Each section should contribute to the maximum its special capabilities in the best interest of the individual.

Design

Just as brains come in different organizational patterns, they also come in different designs. Some brains contain an intricate neural network with many points of connection (synapses). Other brains contain only a simple network with few connection points. Computer scientists find that it is the number of connections rather than the intricacies of the network that determines a computer's capability. Perhaps the same is true of the human brain. Some brains have only one center of control through which all stimuli are channeled. In other brains there are many centers of control available for stimuli processing. The person with a one-track mind may have a brain with only one center of control. Work with laboratory animals has established that sparse neural networks can be developed into more adequate networks and that neural channels that are undesirable can atrophy through disuse. Whether a brain with one control center can develop more control centers remains to be determined.

Goal

Where brain organization is concerned the goal is to have the three sections working together in harmony. Each contributes to the whole its special capabilities. We look to the limbic area for emotion and for the sense of self and relatedness. We look to the right hemisphere for imagination, rhythm, and the dreaming of dreams. We look to the left hemisphere for substantive knowledge, logic, reason, and judgment, as well as for a keen sense of reality and of time. Directing the orchestration is the personucleus—the executive "I"—the source of values, priorities, and goals. To implement values, priorities, and goals the executive "I" has at its service the neural sheath, the overseer making sure that stimuli are channeled to the appropriate section of the brain so that the intent of the executive "I" is realized.

Disharmony in the functioning of the different sections of the brain interferes with the realization of potential. Disharmony can be brought under control—even eliminated—through verbal intervention, as dramatically demonstrated by the BONN approach. BONN is short for brain organization/neural network. The BONN approach is based on brain research findings that have accrued since the 1950s, specifically the findings that deal with (1) what goes on in each of the three sections of the brain—the limbic area, the right hemisphere, and the left hemisphere; and (2) the nature of the neural network: the fact that it can be developed and the fact that neural fibers like muscles can atrophy through disuse.

CHAPTER 2

Neural Network Design: Variations

Neurobiologists David Hubel and Torsten Wiesel in their study of vision found that in the eye some nerve fibers meet while others cross. Damaged nerve fibers can produce incomplete or inaccurate visual perceptions. They found neural pathways from the eye to the brain that signal, link, combine, and fuse stimuli into patterns. They found regions in the eye where stimuli are decoded and where patterns are identified and areas that transmit information to the eye.[3] The variations in neural network design may or may not be flaws depending on how well they serve the eye. Brain researchers, similarly, have found many variations in the design of the brain's neural network.

My clinical experience suggests that there are individuals whose brain design contains in the neural network:

Loops—fibers that end where they begin, the psychological cul-de-sac.

Short circuits—open-ended fibers that end without destination or connection.

Dead ends—fibers with a beginning and an end, not open-ended as the short circuits.

Loose ends—free-floating fibers without anchorage.

Such variations in neural network design affect perception, determining how experiences and knowledge are processed and used.

Brain Design Anomalies

Two young men have provided dramatic clinical evidence of the loop and the dead end in brain design: One, in his early thirties, is married and has two children; the other, in his mid-thirties, is a sexual free-lancer troubled by his lack of interest in committing himself to a relationship but not sufficiently troubled to want to do anything about it. One was a college graduate whose academic performance had been marginal. The other had earned many more course credits than required but not sufficient required credits to earn a degree.

The Loop

The loop or cul-de-sac neural network design is easily recognized. For example, an individual studies a subject and masters it, as measured by established testing procedures. Yet there is no change in the individual's perception, thinking, or behavior. The individual ends where he began. If his preset brain design is right hemisphere-centered, his thinking will remain wholistic, seeing the forest but not being able to distinguish the trees. If his preset brain design is limbic-centered he will have difficulty viewing any point of view that is not consistent with his own. Whether right hemisphere- or limbic-centered, there will be a general absence of concern with reality, time, reason, and logic.

> Rance was an excellent example. In his early thirties, he found himself unemployed, unemployable because his skills had been usurped by the machine. Rance found this reality difficult to understand, impossible to accept. He felt grounded. He did not know where to turn, how to proceed. He had had no experience with pioneering. He was venturesome where science fiction reading was concerned, but not otherwise.
>
> A regime of random reading was prescribed, a search for areas

of interest, areas in which his brain was willing to be involved. Three weeks of extensive reading had taken Rance more deeply into the area from which he had been displaced and in which the future seemed bleak because of technological developments.

Reality had not registered. Rance's reading had been extensive, but it had added nothing to his perception of the world, to his awareness or consideration of the world as it was affecting him. His commitment to what he knew, to what he knew he had to do, to what he was interested in doing, remained unchanged. A looping, a cul-de-sac design in Rance's neural network? Perhaps. If so, was there a way of breaking through it? Could it be changed? There were no ready answers to these questions. They had to be explored. Rance was shocked. He had thought I would be pleased with all he had learned about his field of interest. What he had done was fine if he was not concerned with realities. Was he content to be unemployed, unemployable? Would his family remain intact if he was unable to support them? How long would his resources hold out? Would his wife be willing to be the wage earner while Rance took over the household responsibilities? He was confused. He was frustrated. He was angry. I understood his confusion and his frustration. What Rance had done was important, significant. We had learned something about the way his brain worked that we had no way of knowing before. Rance did have to make a decision: did he want to stay as he was? Did he want to change? I wasn't sure when he left that I would *ever* see him again.

The Dead End

The dead end in the neural network is different from the loop. It is characterized by a forward thrust, that is, it does not go back to where it began. But it doesn't lead anywhere. While the neural fiber has an ending, it doesn't connect with any other fiber. The dead end is an end in itself.

Keith was puzzled; stymied. He knew he was bright. His parents and his teachers had told him so over and over again and tests had validated it. But here he was, thirty-two years old with ten years of postcollege experience behind him and he couldn't even perform adequately a most menial job. He was wondering what life was about. A few months ago he came very close to throwing in the sponge.

Maybe he didn't have what it takes to make it. His floundering made him miserable and was causing his parents great distress.

Keith had heard about me through friends. They were pleased with the results of my new theories and procedures, and they encouraged Keith to talk with me to see if I could help him.

Keith wished he could give some direction to his life. He would like to pursue an education and make better use of his capabilities. But he had been a marginal student, and he doubted that any creditable college would accept him should he ever decide what he would like to study. I explained to Keith my new theories and procedures. His response was immediate, electric. He had had some exposure to brain research findings. He knew about the different sections of the brain. In fact, he had been fascinated by Carl Sagan's *Dragons of Eden*. That these research findings could be translated into ways of dealing with psychological problems had not occurred to him. It was an exciting prospect. He wanted to start right away. There was a problem. Keith didn't know how he could finance the program. We agreed to a deferred-payment plan. Keith would pay me when he could.

In the next interview the pervasiveness and seriousness of Keith's problem became abundantly clear. I estimated that we would need three months of twice-a-week contacts to bring Keith's psychological crisis (and crisis it was) under control. During that time I recommended that he not work. What we were going to undertake to do was going to require all the effort and energy he was likely to have available. Keith had friends with whom he could stay. They would understand if he explained he was in treatment and following the regimen I outlined for him.

Keith's talents were varied. He was a musician, a comedian, an athlete, an artist. He had even written poetry and some short stories. Whatever he did, he did reasonably well but not expertly. He would like some day to be an expert at something.

Quality performance was not possible because Keith had difficulty concentrating. Boredom was something he couldn't tolerate, and he became bored easily. Talent is so misleading, he mused. It holds such promise. The promise comes without effort. How is one to know that to fulfill the promise one must work hard? Not all talented individuals, I explained, are fortunate enough to have teachers who can start where the talent is and build the foundation downward. To start traditionally from the bottom up leads to boredom and often the scuttling or abrogation of talent.

What Keith and I established in this second interview beyond doubt was that Keith was bright, talented, and highly motivated. There was a problem. It had nothing to do with how he was reared. Keith was more than willing to provide me with a detailed litany of what his parents had done to create his present condition. I was not interested.

I believe, as some theorists have proposed, that each individual creates his own history. Each selects out of his life experiences and relationships what makes sense to him according to the mechanisms of perception and reaction with which he comes into the world—that is, according to his own very individual brain organization and design. This brain organization and design is preset by nature. It may be ancestral in pattern. It may be nature's random trial-and-error experimentaion. It may be nature's invention.

In a later interview Keith brought some of his poems and short stories for me to read. They were mediocre. It seemed as though he was scraping the bottom of the barrel of his own knowledge and experience. It was meagre. Nowhere was Keith's college education reflected. I wondered about that. He was not surprised. He had learned what he needed to learn to graduate. He had put no importance on learning. He didn't believe what he learned. He didn't trust it. What Keith had done with education was not unusual. He had done what he was expected to do to achieve his goal. But not for a moment had he relinquished the fantasy of the three-year-old that all he needed to know, all he needed to know how to do, was already stored in his brain. All he had to do was put it to use. Why he had not been able to put it to use when he wanted to, when he needed to, was to Keith a mystery. The mystery was compounded by the fact that everyone said he had special abilities. If so, how come the problem? His conclusion: there was something intrinsically, irreparably wrong with him. This is a conclusion the right hemisphere holds on to tenaciously, often for a lifetime. Since the right hemisphere has no awareness of or concern with reality, it has no way of checking the validity of its conclusions. We do not know how to educate the right hemisphere. We must be content to keep its activities and its conclusions under control. We can do this only if our left hemisphere is fully endowed with (1) knowledge,

(2) the skills of logic, reason, and judgment, and (3) a keen sense of reality and time. For Keith this posed a special problem. It seemed that his left hemisphere was not only poverty stricken, it seemed to be empty. The possibility excited and intrigued Keith. A poverty-stricken, even an empty, left hemisphere was something he could correct.

Keith was eager to get to the library. Once there he found himself paralyzed. He did not know where to start. He went home depressed, concerned that maybe an empty left hemisphere was not as easy to correct as he had thought. As he walked into his parents' home, for the first time he became aware of their library. He browsed. From the many books he chose samples of history, philosophy, science, and a few biographies. There was comfort and reassurance in the preselection his parents had made. He felt safe.

Four weeks passed. They were weeks devoted to reading. Never had Keith been able to stay with any activity for such a long period of time; never had he experienced such internal excitement. It was for him a first; an adventure with many surprises. Keith's family had expected that since Keith was not working he would be able to help with chores and with errands. He did, but he resented the time it took from his project. Keith had not shared with his family what he was doing and why. They were aware of his wanting to be alone. They were delighted with his reading, something he had never done before. They were concerned about the extent to which he was isolating himself, about his lack of social involvement, but they respected it and made minimal demands on his time.

During the four weeks of extensive reading Keith had established to his own satisfaction that he could learn and that he enjoyed learning. With excitement he described the stringent schedule for continued reading which he had set up for himself and the guidelines to check mastery. My reaction: what Keith had done was fine. BUT . . . he was on the verge of transposing the project into an end product, an end in itself. Is that what he had decided to do? My idea had been only to test Keith's ability to learn so that his left hemisphere could be equipped with the knowledge he needed to make decisions. Keith was shocked. He had expected me to be impressed, pleased with what he had outlined for himself. He was utterly and completely confused, exactly as Rance had been when I pointed out his cul-de-sac thinking process, the looping that had brought him back to where he had been.

I made clear to Keith, as I had with Rance, that it was OK to make the project end in itself, but it had serious implications. There was the economic issue. Keith knew if he couldn't work he could go on welfare. He didn't want money to be his sole aim in life, as he saw many people did, but he also didn't want to live at poverty level. He wanted to enjoy his artistic talents; he wanted to add pleasure to the lives of those who were less well endowed than he. Maybe he could write and add to our cultural heritage. He would like to try.

Keith's conclusion: he might become an insurance agent. I was shocked. At no point in any of our discussions had selling been posed as a possibility by Keith. He had made it clear repeatedly that he was not and did not want to be aggressive, as one had to be in a competitive field. I listened carefully, I said nothing, alert for clarification.

Intervention: The Loop and the Dead End

The treatment regime for Rance and Keith had been the same. Their left hemispheres seemed to be devoid of substantive knowledge. They were to involve their brains in random reading in search of areas of interest, areas in which the brain was willing to be involved. Both approached the assignment eagerly. They invested many hours reading. The reading program each developed for himself was markedly different. Rance read in his chosen field, even though it was evident that his chosen field was fast becoming an artifact in today's world. Keith instead undertook a reading program of vast variety—philosophy, science, sociology, archaeology, literature. His mind was a dry sponge. It was open, eager, and ready for anything and everything. There weren't enough hours in the day for Keith to do all he wanted to do. He varied his intellectual diet so that he was not troubled by boredom. He was impressed but not overwhelmed by all there was to know.

Both young men had reached an impasse. For Rance, the reading had led to further entrenchment of what had been previously established. For Keith, reading had opened a new world of vast dimensions to which he wanted to dedicate himself. The new horizons were fine; his excitement was impressive. What was amiss was that the boundaries, the test of mastery, were self-determined. Keith undoubtedly could "make it" according to his own standards. Could he make it in the world of which he was a part? Did he want to construct his own world? Did he want to be a functioning, contributing member of society? Wishing would not make it so, no matter what his right hemisphere did to convince him that it would.

End-of-the-Road or Last-Ditch-Stand

They were difficult days, the days between interviews when I couldn't be certain whether for Rance or Keith we had reached the end of the line or whether the impasse was the proverbial last-ditch-stand not uncommon in clinical experience. Years ago it was generally accepted that people suffering from pneumonia went through a crisis period when life literally hung in the balance. Was it possible that brain redesigning involved a similar period of crisis when the prospect of change was hanging in the balance?

Rance and Keith had both undertaken with enthusiasm and determination the task of correcting the state of poverty that prevailed in their left hemispheres. None of what they learned substantively in college had been distilled for integration or for use. They operated on inherited wisdom. Substantive, conceptualized knowledge was not necessary or important.

As is common for those who operate according to inherited wisdom, they never questioned what they thought. They never concerned themselves with the source of their thinking or feeling. They knew what they knew. It was not open to question. They experienced none of the uncertainty, conflict, or ambivalence of their "egghead" peers who wanted to know the "whys" of everything they encountered. It was unsettling to talk with them. They behaved as though everything were built on quicksand. Rance and Keith saw no advantage to this approach to life and had assiduously avoided it all their lives. This avoidance had led to social isolation, but neither minded that. They had always found most people to be bores. Most of the time they preferred their own company or pursuing their own interests, which were gratifying as solitary pursuits—art, music, and furniture building.

The prospect of converting inherited wisdom into definitive, substantive knowledge was intriguing, even exciting, and certainly a challenge to both Rance and Keith. But was it worth the price? During the past weeks both had tasted intrigue, excitement, and challenge. They were at a point of decision. The preset pattern was still available to them. It was known. It was deeply ingrained. The new pattern required tremendous effort and energy.

There was the uprooting from the old pattern. There was developing and establishing a new pattern. It meant giving up the known for a vast unknown. Could they do it? Was it worth it to try?

I had never promised them a thorn-free rose garden. In fact, at every step I had alerted them to the hazards: commitment to continuing development; preparedness for uncertainty; potential aloneness if they aimed for the stars.

Retreat was their prerogative. I would respect it. Our energies would be redirected. We would concentrate on devising ways for them to make the most of the course they had chosen. I dreaded the thought. Unused potential is a phenomenon I find difficult to accommodate. For these two young men I knew the retreat would be difficult, one that neither would accommodate easily.

My worry had been needless but not without cause. The next interview marked a change. Never had Rance looked so handsome and well put together. His eyes sparkled. A wonderful thing had happened over the weekend. He had heard of a job opening. It was a field in which he had neither knowledge nor experience, but he could learn. He was prepared to give the interview all he had.

Rance wanted me to know that our last interview had "thrown" him. He left it utterly confused. He was intensely angry. He almost decided not to come to see me today. I was not surprised. Rance had obviously heard all that I had said as well as what I had not said. He had been at the crossroads. He had had to choose.

As we reviewed our total experience with the brain design/neural network approach, what was interesting was that even if Rance had decided not to proceed, the original gains had at no point been in jeopardy:

He no longer had difficulty getting up in the morning, nor did he greet the day with anger.

He continued to organize his day and rarely aborted his schedule.

His memory was no longer giving him trouble, nor did he have difficulty concentrating. If interferences from the right hemi-sphere and limbic areas, occurred, as they occasionally did, they were readily and easily brought under control. Rance's exuberance had no bounds. He seemed to be seeing every-thing—people, situations, things—for the first time, appreciating them in a new way. It was like being born again.

Keith was less exuberant but none the less clear. Whether he went to work or to school, it would be difficult. Effort would be involved in his becoming a responsible employee. He would have to learn to get along with management and his co-workers. Keith decided that he would prefer to put his energies into advancing his knowl-edge so that he could eventually become the scientist he would like to be. He knew this would not be easy. First, Keith was not sure any educational institution would consider him for advanced study in the light of his mediocre undergraduate record.

Keith decided he would investigate the possibility of furthering his education. At the same time, he would arrange to take a battery of tests to determine whether his dream of becoming a scientist was a realistic one or whether the arts were a more appropriate field for him. Keith understood more clearly than ever before how in-complete his selfhood was. He had not yet severed the psycholog-ical umbilical cord from his parents. He was better. But they still had too strong a hold on him. As far as authenticity was concerned, he was reasonably clear as to his range of interests and talents. What he had not done was to decide which talents he wanted to develop first. This was why he decided to take the psychological battery. Perhaps the results would help him with the decision.

Other Anomalies

The Short Circuit

Alicia was an enigma to her therapist, her family, and her friends. She had graduated with a four-point average from a prestigious East Coast university known for its high academic standards. She had been one of five in a class of 250 selected for a combined program in the humanities. Alicia had been unimpressed with the special privilege of a combined program. She was even less impressed with her grade-point average. Her professors didn't know what she didn't know. It was what she didn't know that overwhelmed Alicia. This made her college experience of little significance to her.

In social situations Alicia sought out the most accomplished of her peers. She asked them searching questions, eager to know all about them, their interests, and their accomplishments. She shared little if anything about herself. Her questions were naïve. There was nothing in her social participation that gave any indication of her knowledge and achievements. Her knowledge seemed to be stored in separate cubicles. It could be brought into play only with conscious effort. And Alicia avoided that.

As the neural network theory of intervention became available, Alicia was advised that perhaps there were in her neural network some short circuits. Knowledge was acquired and stored. There appeared to be no connecting links, no synapses joining network fibers so that knowledge could flow into and out of different channels as the situation required.

Alicia was angry. No one had ever suggested there was anything wrong with her brain. Though she had always had a great deal of confidence in her therapist, who had seen her through many crises, she was not about to consider the theory, let alone accept it. She knew it was a new theory. She knew her therapist was posing it only as a possibility.

A few weeks later Alicia and her therapist met in a social situation. There was a marked difference in Alicia's participation. She was more spontaneous. More striking than that was her reminiscing about her childhood and her experiences as a cheerleader in junior high school. There was an element of pride in her account that had never been present either socially or in therapy.

The change was apparent also in the next therapeutic session. Questions went through the therapist's mind. Was Alicia's brain so affronted by the thought that there might be something wrong with it that there was spontaneous correction? Could just the suggestion of a possible lack establish a previously nonexistent bridge? Is it possible that the bridge had always been there but had been blocked or just not used?

Alicia provided the answer. After our last discussion she remembered. When she was thirteen her family had moved to a new area. Her new teacher criticized the way she approached problems and the way she drew comparisons and contrasts. She had always been praised for her problem-solving skill. Alicia was confused. She just stopped using her brain. During the rest of her school experience she learned what she had to know without thinking.

With Lori, there was a short circuiting of another type. Lori was a vivacious young woman in her late thirties. She was well read. Her interests were varied, and her enthusiasm about each of them was infectious. She was the life of the party. People sought Lori out to go on hikes and excursions. Lori was delighted to be sought after, but preferred going places alone. She enjoyed her own company. No one meeting Lori in a social situation would have any inkling of the major frustration in her life—the fact that she was a poor student.

Lori's dream from early childhood had been that she would be a "somebody," a somebody people would respect and admire. She loved to read but it was difficult. Her eyes kept jumping back and forth between the lines. Reading was a tedious process.

Lori's grades were usually good, not excellent, as everyone expected them to be. Every assignment was torture. No matter how many papers Lori had written, each paper loomed as though it were a first. She didn't know how to begin. She did not know how to proceed once she had begun. Alicia's knowledge was in separate boxes. Lori's achievements were dead-ended. They led to their destination but there was no linkage to other tasks. The knowledge and skill she acquired from one activity did not generalize. No matter how many times Lori had done a task before, it seemed to her that she was doing it for the first time.

Procedures for correcting the short circuiting were developed. First, Lori's eyes had to be retrained so that reading was not hampered by back-and-forth movement. A fifteen-minute daily regimen of reading—not for content or comprehension but only to exercise the eyes to follow the printed lines sequentially—brought the reading problem under control in a few weeks.

A more extensive reading regimen followed. Exploration of Lori's learning pattern had revealed that she could not distinguish between a description and a rule, between a fact and a possibility. Therefore, she could not determine what was essential and what was incidental to the assigned task. Consequently, her learning was unfocused and disorganized.

To correct these anomalies three steps were designed:

1. Read the material under consideration for an overview.
2. Reread. Code each sentence to designate whether it is
   a. Description.
   b. Instruction—procedure.
   c. A rule to be learned by rote.
   d. Explanation; clarification; extrapolation.
3. Outline, using as headings the above categories.

In less than three months the anomalies were corrected. Reading was no longer a problem. Lori's eyes were trained not to jump back and forth between lines. She had learned quickly to distinguish between description, instruction, a rule, and extrapolation. Her note taking as she read was appropriately selective and organized. Generalizing from one task to another had begun. Lori considered taking a math course to see if that would give her the necessary experience and practice with generalization. On the basis of these achievements Lori undertook a postgraduate program and graduated with honors for the first time in her educational experience. It was difficult. The old problems would surface. She had to be on constant alert. She had to be ready on a moment's notice to reinstitute the practice procedures so that the old patterns did not once again become entrenched. Lori was alert, disciplined, and determined. She has had objective evidence of her learning potential and is already taking the next steps toward the realization of her childhood dream.

Loose Ends

The BONN approach to personality and behavior is casting into new light personality phenomena long known to the clinician. There have been the "as if" personality, which takes on the coloration and behavior of the individuals with whom the person is in contact; the dependent personality, which lacks self-direction and motivation; the psychopathic personality, which seems to be without guilt and anxiety, without internalized standards of behavior. It has been assumed over the years that these types of individuals received inadequate nurturing and socialization in their formative years.

The BONN theory poses the possibility that these conditions might instead be the result of preset brain design, the fault of no one, the responsibility of nature. It also poses the strong possibility of personality modification, so that impaired individuals may be able to function more effectively in society.

At age three, Sherry was without fear. She wandered into water beyond her depth and experienced no panic when she lost her balance. In shopping malls she wandered far from her mother. At eighteen, Sherry was a gun moll sitting in a courtroom ready to shoot on signal. There was no concern for consequences, no awareness of cause-effect, no sense of right or wrong. Sherry had been a much-loved first child and grandchild. She was beautiful and bright. There was nothing in her life experience to account for her out-of-control, unmanageable behavior and reactions.

At age twenty-four Sherry had many friends. In fact, she had different groups of friends. Each group was special. Her mood determined her choice. There was the group that went to bars. There was the group that invited danger—speeding, racing, stealing. There was the group that enjoyed dinner and talk. Whether Sherry intended it or not, she found herself on center stage, the life of the party. If she had too much to drink she could be obnoxious. Her friends seemed to think her behavior was funny. On one recent occasion Sherry found herself doing and saying things she didn't mean to people who were important to her. Suddenly she was frightened. For the first time she realized that if she lost control she could hurt someone, or herself. She would never want to do that. This experience brought her into treatment.

Our discussions were illuminating. Sherry really didn't know who she was. Her family, friends, and teachers had told her she was pretty and bright. She had no sense of being pretty. She gave little thought to her hair or to the clothes she wore. How she looked wasn't important. What was important? Sherry didn't know. There were times when she was very sorry that her marriage of seven years had failed. It would have been nice if she and Dan had been able to grow together. But marriage was so dull. They never did anything interesting or exciting. And then when Wayne was born their world fell apart. Sherry wasn't ready to take care of a baby. She couldn't tolerate his fussiness. Her anger was intense when he wakened her. She was afraid her anger would get out of control and she would hurt him. She contacted an agency. They arranged for his placement in a foster home where he is doing well. Sherry visits him regularly.

There were few things Sherry had done that gave her a good feeling. Arranging for Wayne to be well taken care of was one of those few. Sherry wasn't sure that she was bright. Her family often reminisced about her brilliance as a preschooler. With little effort she had done outstanding work in school. She had done little work at school. She believes she was graduated not on the basis of what she had achieved but on the basis of her assessed potential. Sherry liked to be with people who were bright and knowledgeable. Yet she avoided them because she felt inadequate in their presence.

Sherry reported that her family had been troubled about her as far back as she could remember. They had urged her to have therapy. She thought it was they who needed therapy, not she. She was adamant in her refusal. Her decision to come to see me was based on three things: her best friends no longer wanted to have anything to do with her; she had panicked when she realized that her behavior could get out of control and she might hurt herself or persons important to her. Finally, she had heard about me and my new procedures based on current brain research from people who had been helped. She wanted to find out if there was anything I could do for her.

I marveled aloud that Sherry was still alive. She agreed. She told me of the close calls she had experienced in a race car contest and the speed chase by the police when her companions were interrupted in a robbery attempt. As a gun moll, it had not occurred to her that it was extremely dangerous to sit in a court room with gun cocked to shoot at the signal of her friend who was on trial. As a matter of fact, she never thought about consequences. When she responded angrily to her friends it often was without obvious cause. She didn't know where the anger came from. She didn't know why her friends put up with her. She didn't know why they had changed recently. They have refused to tolerate her anger and her aggressiveness. They went so far as to put her out when her behavior got out of line, leaving her to her own resources. This has happened twice. Each time Sherry panicked. She realized she had no place to go and no one to turn to.

For the first time in ten years Sherry turned to her family. They still loved her. She could return home, but only on one condition—that she have help. Sherry knew this was what they would expect. She agreed without qualification.

Fortunately, Sherry's ego was sufficiently intact (contact with reality) that she realized things were getting out of control and she needed help if she was to survive.

I explained to Sherry my theory of brain organization and neural network design. From her description of her life experience it seemed to me that she did not have a self. She did not have a sense of being whole and separate. She did not have a sense that others are whole and separate—that just as she is an "I," so everyone else is a separate "I," unique and distinct. Sherry's eyes opened wide. They shown brilliantly. Sherry was obviously unbelieving. She had never realized that. No wonder she was always taken aback when others didn't agree with her. No wonder she always felt so threatened. Every disagreement was an attack. Every disapproval shook her to the very foundation.

Suddenly Sherry realized how lucky she was that she had friends who cared about her. Maybe they always knew that she cared about them and that she would never, under any circumstances, intentionally hurt them. Maybe her family knew this too. Even though months might go by when she had no contact with them, they always seemed pleased to hear from her. She knew that if she ever asked their help they would be there. What Sherry was saying seemed a revelation to her. She had never thought about these things. She had experienced them; taken them for granted. She was intrigued by the possibility that she had never been "bad."

Our discussion apparently had an immediate effect. Sherry's mother telephoned the next morning. What had I done to Sherry? Sherry had called after she had talked with me. There was something dramatically different in Sherry's tone of voice and in what she said and how she said it. Sherry's mother was delighted and unbelieving. It seemed to her that suddenly she had a daughter she didn't know. She was eager to make her acquaintance.

Five months have passed. Sherry continues to be an involved, responsible member of the family. On only two occasions did she fail to call her parents when she was unable to come home as planned. She makes plans for the time she spends with her son and is more resourceful in the use of that time. For the first time she is working full time and has received her first promotion and salary increase.

Three months of weekly interviews brought us to this point. Treatment will be resumed when I return to practice. Focus will be on further development of the left hemisphere—the building of knowledge, logic, reason, and judgment as they relate to reality. There is every evidence that what we are doing is proceeding well. Sherry has given up her antisocial friends and is beginning to be more discriminating in her selection of the individuals with whom she spends her free time. That her family is pleased with her present friends is a significant indicator.

Sherry's job is comparatively simple. We can anticipate that being as bright as she is, Sherry will find the job dull as soon as she has fully mastered the basic issues of being punctual, dependable, and responsible. The focus then will be on her potential, with the major question being what she would like to do with her life. Sherry has ruled out marriage. That is not where she wants to put her energies. She finds that the person most important in her life is her son. She thinks she would like to resume parenthood. She isn't sure. She knows that to be a good mother she has to be sure of who she is and know her own values, priorities, and goals. She wants to work on this area so that she can be self-motivating, no longer a pawn on a chessboard subject to the whims and machinations of others. The prognosis is excellent.

Many questions remain unanswered. Why did the idea of the separate self bring about such dramatic results in one interview? Was there something amiss in the way the neural fibers in Sherry's limbic section were strung or organized or connected? Was there no neural connection between the limbic area and the left hemisphere, so that reality had no way of getting through to the limbic area for processing or registering? Something other than nurturance, socialization, and school experience must have been awry. That correction was possible so quickly is impressive. It warrants exploration and testing. It holds promise for change far beyond that available with the nurturance, socialization, and educational experience frame of reference.

Jane's situation seemed to contain some of the same elements as Sherry's. But there were significant differences.

It was our first meeting. Jane's parents had insisted she see me. At sixteen Jane looked twenty and had begun to behave as if she were thirty. She acted as though she not only knew all the answers but knew best. She was failing all of her courses, though she planned to go to college. She wanted to be a professional athlete but was beginning to do poorly in her athletic program. There was the beginning of delinquent behavior—disrespect for curfew, carelessness with family property, and a general indifference to family expectations. Jane claimed not to know why her parents were upset about her. She was old enough to know what was right, especially what was right for herself. She thought her performance at school was "all right," although she was failing.

The quality of Jane's responses was in the dull–normal range. Knowing her family as I did, it did not seem likely that she would be low in intelligence. My mind was on the alert—was there a break with reality?

I explained that Jane's mother had been concerned about her for some time and that I had suggested Jane come to see me. I wanted to tell her about my new discoveries based on brain research and to see whether we could locate the source of her problems.

Jane's interest was immediate. Her eyes sparkled, and at times she sat on the edge of her chair listening intently to every word. It was all new to her. It made sense. Her conclusion was that the interactions in her brain were complex and confusing. Her brain worked so differently from any others in the family. She had often wondered whether she had inherited a brain different from the others, or whether there was something wrong with her brain. I pointed out the vagaries of nature—the fact that nature can replicate and invent by trial and error or by design. Jane knew that nature seems in constant search for improvements.

The way Jane responded to what I said was indisputable evidence that she was not dull—that, in fact, she was bright, perhaps extremely so.

In this first interview we did not get into whether her brain's neural network contained loops, dead ends, or short circuits. From her response to the information there seemed to be no doubt in her mind that Jane thought there were. We discussed the preset pattern of her brain, with which she had been born, the archaic sections, and the fact that her limbic area and right hemisphere seemed to be in control. Her left hemisphere, well endowed though it was, was inoperative. It was clear from our discussion that Jane had accumulated much knowledge during her sixteen years but that it was not being used. If she was willing to see me again, we would check whether something was amiss in the neural network so that the knowledge in the left hemisphere was not getting through to the limbic section and the right hemisphere.

Jane was thoughtful. Yes, she would come back. I gave her an assignment. I needed to know who she was. I asked for an inventory of her likes and dislikes, interests, and aptitudes and lacks. I wanted to have an idea of how Jane planned to go about becoming a professional athlete, or tour guide or designer, before she settled for marriage and children, as she said she wanted to do.

Jane was surprised when I spoke of her size as a handicap. She protested. The people in her life knew how old she was. She was sure they didn't expect more of her than was appropriate for a sixteen-year-old. I told her I had had to keep reminding myself that she was only sixteen. Her appearance, manner, sensitivity, and awareness fit more with age twenty than age sixteen. I was sure people expected a great deal of Jane that was related to how she looked and responded than to her actual age. Jane was fascinated. No one had ever said anything like that to her before. It was an interesting perspective as far as she was concerned.

I wasn't sure Jane would return. She didn't. There were important issues to be dealt with. I saw Jane's parents. Since Jane's perceptions of reality seemed to be inaccurate and inadequate (consider her unawareness of problem behavior), her parents needed to make sure that she heard and understood them. They were to take nothing for granted. Everything was to be spelled out.

If Jane continued to ignore the curfew, she would not be permitted use of the car. This undoubtedly would mean she would have to give up her weekend job.

If Jane continued unable to learn, she could get a part-time work permit and go to school only part-time.

If she continued to borrow from her mother's wardrobe without permission and to return the articles in a condition other than the way they were when she took them, her mother would assume that she had acquired them as her own and would expect to be reimbursed for them.

In these procedures there was no intent to punish. It was important that the conditions be set without anger or criticism—just statements of fact and clarification of realities. Jane's left hemisphere needed as much reinforcement as possible where time and reality were concerned. Her parents could help. The underlying message Jane's parents needed to communicate was that she was only sixteen. The responsibilities she had taken on were probably too much for her. It was OK for her not to work and not drive a car. It was OK if she didn't continue her schooling. Anytime she was ready to learn she would be able to. She had a very able brain.

Network Overload

One needs to be ever on the alert for overextension.

Beth had had a wonderful year. Her fourteenth birthday had been extra special. Relatives had come from abroad and fallen in love with her, and for good reason. She was a charming, delightful, sensitive, and thoughtful young woman, in some ways wiser than you would have expected for her age.

At school Beth had blossomed into a leader much sought after by her peers. She had done a solo in a concert. She had had the semi-lead in a play. She had been elected to the student government. And she was a much-in-demand babysitter.

Then something began to happen. Her school work slipped. She continued as a leader but in disruptive activities. She was not re-elected to student government. She was not out of control at home, but she was not following the rules.

Beth had a boyfriend. The lengthy chatting on the phone with her girl friends gave evidence of growing preoccupation with boy-girl issues. Her mother was watching this behavior closely, linking responsibility and privilege in an effort to avoid exposure and stimulation that might be more than Beth could handle.

The day Beth failed to telephone to tell her mother that she would be home late was the day her mother decided she needed to do something. Babysitting seemed to be the most appropriate point of intervention, since babysitting was so clearly a matter of responsibility.

Beth wept inconsolably when her mother told her that until she proved herself to be more responsible, she was not to accept baby-sitting jobs. And then an amazing change took place. Beth was sober. Would her mother call the family for whom she sat regularly and who liked her so much? Of course. Beth's face clouded. She needed so many things for school now that a new semester was starting. That was OK. They would go shopping together to make sure Beth had all she needed.

And then came a flood of questions. Which of her friends did her mother like best? What did she like about them? Beth wasn't sure whom she preferred. And of course there were those who didn't like her. A new closeness was present.

Had babysitting been too much responsibility for Beth? Had she perhaps been frightened to be alone in a big house with a young child dependent on her? She had never given any indication of this. But being relieved of the responsibility seemed to make it OK for her to be a child again, looking for guidance and reassurance, looking for the support a fourteen-year-old in our society has a right to expect of caring, nurturing parents. Limits need to be seen as a language of "caring" and not punishment. They need to reflect the child's demonstrated mastery of responsibility before further responsibility is added, even when the new responsibility is masked as privilege (like driving a car).

Many years ago, long before I had discovered the findings of brain research and before I had undertaken the arduous, solitary task of implementing the findings, Anita came to my office on referral from her professor at a prestigious eastern college. She had registered at the local college in order to be able to work with me. She was a senior. She had completed all of her requirements and was now taking only electives, the subjects she liked most. At nineteen, that was an achievement. She was not impressed. School was no problem. Relationships were.

Anita was sure she wanted help. She wasn't sure I was the right person. She asked about my background, my theories, my philosophy, and what I saw as the goal of treatment. I answered her questions as completely and as forthrightly as I could. I explained the structure of my service. At that time I required that if an individual went beyond the first interview, there was a commitment to four visits. This constituted the diagnostic period. At the end of four interviews I expected that Anita would know whether I was being helpful. And I would know whether she was using our discussions appropriately. We together could decide where to go from there. Beyond the four interviews there was only one commitment. If Anita decided to end by individual rather than mutual decision, she would come in for a final interview so that we could tie together any loose ends and assess what if anything had been accomplished. Anita was thoughtful. She seemed to be weighing the conditions and considering the implications. She agreed to the four interviews.

The second interview was a dynamic one. Anita was fully and excitedly involved in sorting out her life experiences and the significance they had had for her. She was perceptive, sensitive, and insightful. Her potential for treatment in short order seemed excellent.

Had I not been a practitioner of wide experience, well aware that a quick moving in can be the forerunner of quick withdrawal, I would have been completely thrown by Anita in the third interview. She sat on the edge of the chair clutching her coat. She had made a decision. She would not go ahead with treatment. She realized after our second interview that her whole life was dependent upon her problems. She would not know how to get along without them. Anita was distressed by her decision. Did I think she would ever be able to change? I was reassuring without qualification. Anita would be able to change whenever she decided to do so. The important thing would be that she find a therapist in whom she could have confidence.

The interview lasted no more than ten minutes. There was no charge. Anita left. I never saw or heard from her again. Never up to that time or since have I experienced such sadness. What a shame that she could not risk change. Hopefully one day she would be able to, for without it her vast potential was not likely to be realized.

Had the brain organization/neutral network (BONN) approach been available, Anita would not have been thrown into a panic by the prospect of an early resolution to her problems. She would have experienced, as every individual does, the feeling of being in control, of being able to decide which part of the brain is to be in charge. Anita would have learned immediately that her problems came from the archaic limbic section of her brain. She would have been able to understand quickly why being as bright and knowledgeable as she was made no difference in her behavior. The reason was that very likely the neural connections between her left hemisphere and the limbic system were either nonexistent or few in number, as is true of many brains. She would have been relieved of any worry about pathology either in her system or in her life experiences and relationships. She would have been provided with the procedures for constructing or developing the neural connections between the left hemisphere and the limbic section.

The procedures are simple. They require practice. The limbic section is educable with techniques we know. This is not true of the right hemisphere. The most we can do with current understanding and skills is to keep the right hemisphere under control and allow it to find its own ways of being a cooperative, complementary force in the brain complex.

The therapeutic task concerning Anita would have been a relatively simple one even with the use of what I called maturational therapy. It would have been simpler and faster and attended by less panic with the BONN frame of reference.

Neural Network Insufficiency: Smoking, Drinking, and Overeating

Where neural network insufficiency is concerned no more graphic evidence can be imagined than that reflected in the prevalence of smoking, drinking, and overeating in our society. We are bombarded by mounting evidence, physical and pyschological, of the risks to survival posed by tobacco, alcohol, and intemperate appetite. There is even a social dimension to these individual behaviors:

The smoke of tobacco is hazardous to nonsmokers.
Alcohol in its effect on behavior endangers relationships.
Intemperate eating places life at risk and in so doing subjects those who care to the suffering of loss through illness or death.

Yet smoking, drinking, and overeating persist. The left hemisphere has the knowledge. Apparently what is lacking is the neural circuitry to carry the knowledge to the limbic section where the "I want" holds sway.

The despair people experience when their repeated efforts to curb the destructive behavior fail attests to the fact that the behavior is not within the realm of conscious control. It is not a matter of faulty goals or commitment.

Neural Network Development

The executive "I" tried to assert its authority based on its values, priorities, and goals, but finds its authority blocked by an inadequate transmission system. What the left hemisphere knows that is consistent with executive "I" aims has no way of getting through to the offending section. The offending section knows nothing of knowledge, logic, reason, or judgment but functions solely on inherited wisdom, instinct, reflex, habit.

Once there is a neural channel between left hemisphere and the limbic section, knowledge, logic, judgment, and reality can be transmitted to the limbic area—the decision made by the "I." The decision is firm. No longer is the limbic area permitted to promote behavior that is destructive to the well-being of the individual. The firmness of the left hemisphere position is reinforced by determination reflected in consistency. Where smoking is concerned consistency requires follow-through on three steps:

1. The left hemisphere must be on constant alert for the impulse to smoke. Once the impulse takes hold it is difficult to interrupt.

2. As soon as the left hemisphere recognizes the impulse it must relay the information on smoking and the decision to stop smoking to the limbic area—clearly and firmly. There is no room for disagreement or dissent; an order is called for.

3. If the limbic section pays no attention and persists in the "want," the individual must stop whatever he or she is doing and do something else. If driving, change course, consciously and deliberately. Or if listening to the radio, change the station. The brain can concentrate on only one thing at a time. Changing the point of con-

centration cuts the flow of energy from the original source. If this is done often enough the offending neural channel will atrophy and the impulse to maladaptive behavior will be eliminated.

With overeating the procedure is essentially the same, but the context is different. Individuals wanting to change their eating behavior to control their weight must follow one step preceding the above. They must be sure that they have a regular eating schedule they follow whether they are hungry or not. At each meal they must make sure that what they eat is adequate to meet nutritional requirements. With these two conditions met, hunger based on nutritional needs does not exist. Hunger, if it registers, comes from needs other than biological. The "on the alert" stance is the same for the smoker, drinker, and overeater. The content of the message from the left hemisphere is different. The limbic section must be reminded it has had adequate food. It must be reminded that eating is to meet the nutritional needs of the body. No other reason is valid. No other reason will be tolerated. This position is consistent with the decision of the executive "I" in the interest of whatever values, priorities, and goals had led the "I" to decide to change.

If the limbic area persists in its demand for food, the overeater, like the smoker, must stop what he or she is doing and do something else. The alert, the determination not to be victim to an uninformed, archaic impulse that is placing one's life at risk must be firm, consistent, and unfailing. Only under those conditions can a new channel be developed.

Summary: Part I

The BONN approach to personality and behavior has a dual focus:

> *The organization of the brain:* which section is in control—the limbic area, the locus of emotions; the right hemisphere, the locus of fantasy and imagination; the left hemisphere, the locus of knowledge, logic, reason, judgment, reality, and time perception?

The neural network design: how adequate is it, and what anomalies exist between the sections and within each section? Are there adequate neural channels to carry knowledge from the left hemisphere to the right hemisphere and limbic area? Are the existing channels encumbered by loops, short circuits, dead ends, and loose ends that interfere with the free flow of data within each section and between sections?

The BONN approach carries a specific and firm bias: for species survival and for individuals to realize their maximum potential in a mobile, technologically sophisticated world, it is essential that the left hemisphere be in control—that knowledge, logic, reason, and judgment supersede emotions and imagination in the management of reality and time.

Left hemisphere control requires for direction, for the selection of values and the setting of goals, a firmly rooted executive "I." A firmly rooted executive "I" requires a self that is autonomous and authentic, with a clear sense of its place with and among people (society) and in the universe. It is with the characteristics of self that Part II will be concerned.

PART II

THE CENTRALITY of SELF

CHAPTER 3

The Self: Structure, Content, Function

The BONN approach to personality and behavioral change has brought into sharp focus the importance of the phenomenon commonly referred to as the "self." Apples have cores. Cherries have pits. Wheels have hubs. The earth has an axis. These are essential organizing elements of each system. Similarly, the brain in its personality/behavior context requires a unifying, governing, and directing unit if its component parts are to function in harmony.

The Personucleus

The personucleus, like the blueprint of body structure, musculature, and organ capability, comes with conception. It is the seed to self. Boundaries with outer limits, potentials in vast variety are blueprinted in the seed. The blueprint carries promise, not prediction. It comes with no guarantee. Why some personuclei reach full fruition while others remain at the seedling stage remains a mystery. The most we can do at the present level of our knowledge and skill is to observe, assemble our observations, look for patterns, tentative though they may be, and develop procedures for dealing with those patterns that are dysfunctional.

The Self: Variations

Selves vary widely from one to the other. The variations can be in *structure*, *content*, and *function*. Selves carry the mark of hemisphere dominance and are affected by neural network design. Five types of selves will be examined: the full-blown self; the in-tandem self; the encapsulated self; the surrendered self; and the in-limbo self. The in-tandem self and the encapsulated self are viewed as having structural faults. The in-limbo self is seen as being the result of a fault in neural network design. The surrendered self reflects a fault in content. Whatever the nature of its fault, each type of self is amenable to change through the BONN approach. As in all other conditions requiring change, there must be commitment to change. The commitment can be internally motivated by experienced discomfort. It can also be externally motivated by the exigencies of reality. The commitment to change can be supported and strengthened by clarity as to the nature of the task, the procedures to be followed, and the goals to be achieved. Left hemisphere involvement—knowledge, logic, reason, and judgment—is the primary essential requisite. Content and function are adjustable to individual need and capability.

The Full-Blown Self: A Yardstick

Four characteristics mark the full-blown self: autonomy, authenticity, accessibility, and actualization.

> Autonomy—a sense of wholeness, completeness.
> Authenticity—clarity as to values, priorities, and goals; a sense of the "real me."
> Accessibility—availability to individuals, groups, and community, consistent with values, priorities, and goals.
> Actualization—pursuit of maximum potential consistent with values, priorities, and goals.

The full-blown self has boundaries. It knows where it begins and ends and where others begin and end. It knows what it knows or at least can consider for action what it would like to be able to do and to what end. The full-blown self has a sense of its own individuality together with a sense of commonality. It has achieved separateness without isolation. It has achieved individuation within the broad context of togetherness, an at-oneness with others, with community, and with the cosmos in a broad, philosophical sense.

Hopefully, as we become more knowledgeable about the brain and how it functions, the full-blown self, realization of human potential will become a commonplace. Society can direct its efforts to that end.

The In-Tandem Self

In the in-tandem self one finds dramatic evidence of Otto Rank's contention. A protegé of Freud, Rank believed that no one recovers from the trauma of birth. One might add to this the possibility that the human organism never gives up the wish and the hope that the experiences of the nine-month intrauterine stage will once again exist. This wish explains the perennial search for the two-makes-one relationship; the situation in which one's wants and needs are satisfied without one's knowing one has wants and needs; and the persistent longing for security and safety without qualification or reservation.

The persistence of the wish, the search, and the longing suggests that the psychological umbilical cord does not automatically self-destruct as does the physical umbilical cord. The prolonged dependency required by the human organism gives nurturance to the psychological umbilical cord. The world we live in gives nurturance to the fantasy that what we once had still exists and is available. The frequent changing of partners because no one quite measures up to expectations is evidence of the persistence of the fantasy the roots of which lie in the womb experience.

The in-tandem personality is neither rare nor difficult to identify. It is found among those who are reluctant to go alone to restaurants, theaters, hotels, or on travels. Women seem more prone to hesitation in these activities than men. Here may be reflected the effect of couple culture to which unattached women are so sensitive.

The in-tandem personality may be suspected in the newly separated man or woman who immediately begins to "play the field." One may suspect it also in the newly singled who, suffering loss as a consequence of divorce or death, immediately begin the search for a replacement. Loss is often not allowed to register and certainly not allowed to heal. New relationships suffer. They become victimized by unsuffered loss, unresolved guilt, and unresolved anger. A television talk show guest put it succinctly: "No one is perfect; except my wife's first husband." What a sober, touching observation!

The Encapsulated Self

The encapsulated self has a unique characteristic. It views its own world as the whole world. It is unaware of variations or deviations. To the encapsulated self there is only one way—indeed only one right way.

The anomaly is structural. The encapsulated self has fixed, rigid boundaries. They are limited to and by the individual's perceptions. The individual expects everyone to see people, things, and situations as he does. He has no awareness that each individual is a separate, distinct entity with his own view of people, things, and situations and his own system of values, priorities, and goals. The encapsulated self views itself as universal and its unilateral reactions as absolute and beyond question. When face to face with difference, the individual with an encapsulated self feels under attack, his very existence at risk. He is ever ready to attack in self defense (psychotic) or withdraw into his self-boundaried world, desolate and isolated.

It was our twelfth interview. Tim became thoroughly exasperated. There was no use talking to me. I didn't listen. I didn't hear. I didn't understand. I leaned back in my chair, conceding by implication that this might well be so. Certainly, Tim had a right to his perceptions. He instantly caught the significance of my reaction. He didn't have to continue to come. I would be sorry if he terminated treatment, but I would understand.

Tim leaned forward in his chair and began to recount the changes that had occurred since he began talking with me. He almost never makes his brother angry. (This had been confirmed by his mother.) They almost never quarrel. If they do, it is usually because Tim has misunderstood what Phil had said. There was no longer a problem about food. His mother told him what he might have for snacks. It helps him to know. There was something else. Tim's face lit up as he told me there were times when he helped his mother (confirmed by family). Tim's school work had improved. He was having more fun with his classmates. He had transferred from football to a general athletic program, which he loves.

Separateness, his own and others', the realities of living in a family and in society—these were the facts introduced to the left hemisphere for use in whittling away at Tim's encapsulated self. Frequent repetition was the process by which the channel from the left hemisphere to the limbic area was developed so that left hemisphere knowledge could be brought to bear on the limbic misperceptions that had led to the fixed, rigid boundaries of encapsulation.

The nineteenth interview brought objective evidence of the break-through. Tim was on time. (He usually was five to ten minutes late because he delayed getting up and he dawdled.) There was a jauntiness to his step as he came into the room. Never had his hair been so carefully combed. Never had his face looked so scrubbed. Tim couldn't wait to show me what he had done. His pride in himself knew no bounds. He watched closely for my reactions to his two-page statement entitled, "How To Be a Student." It read:

"You know I'm a student because . . . I go to school every day (except weekends) and try to learn as much as I can. In English I wasn't doing well so I sat away from my friends, and got to class as early as I could.

Some things you should concentrate on if you're a student are as follows:

1. Try to get along with the teacher.
2. Try your hardest to accomplish goals set for the grading period.
3. Be neat when doing math, taking tests, etc.
4. Don't give up on yourself even if others do.

There are many more things you should concentrate on. I will mention only one more, the most important one: respect your teacher, friends, and other students as well as yourself."

Here was impressive summation of our accomplishments, and they have held.

The Surrendered Self

The surrendered self reflects a fault in content. Separateness and awareness of others have been achieved. The gap is ideational. The individual is not clear as to the rights that come with being alive, the privileges inherent in being a separate, whole, unique human being, with abilities and potentials, the endowment of nature. The poet Milton paid tribute to the surrendered self in his poem "On Blindness": "They also serve who only stand and wait." To be sure. For some individuals there may well be a specialness in being "on call." There may be special gratification in living in reflected glory or in helping others reach their goals and maximize their potentials.

When being "on call" results in a feeling of "forgive me for living" —the proverbial "doormat" sensation—and when it adds up to the frustration of being taken for granted, the surrendered self is an aborted self. Its potential lies fallow. Its generosity is unrewarded except as in itself it brings gratification.

There are people who derive pleasure from giving pleasure to others. There are people who treasure the privilege of having others to love. These rare individuals give with no strings attached, without expectation of return. Being in a position to give is to them a gift, a source of self-esteem and joy in living. They may have the outer trappings of the surrendered self. But in essence they are full-blown selves that have reached the highest level of human experience.

The In-Limbo Self

The in-limbo self is an enigma. The individual, often bright, talented, educated, and experienced, stands out as volatile, inconsistent, and lacking in self-awareness and awareness of others.

In traditional clinical practice such an individual has been known as the "as if" personality, kaleidoscopic, taking on the characteristics of those with whom he or she happens to be. The individuality of such persons—if it exists—is dissipated, submerged by the influence of others. They can find themselves at home with intellectuals and with criminals with equal aplomb.

Other patterns that fall within the in-limbo self category have been known in traditional clinical practice as the psychopath who experiences no guilt or anxiety and the individual who is devoid or unaware of feeling.

The in-limbo self acts. It reacts. It experiences. Nothing registers in its consciousness, and nothing generalizes from one situation to another. Stimuli–response is its pattern, with no concern for cause and effect or for cost or consequence; no recognition or acceptance of responsibility; and no sense of participation. Mechanical, automaton-like behavior characterizes best its pattern of operation.

The fault in such individuals lies in the neural network design of the limbic section. The network contains many loose ends or free-floating fibers. Hence the self is without foundation or boundaries, open-ended and subject to whatever influences dominate the moment.

Cheryl's turmoil ridden life is a prime example.

At twenty-eight Cheryl had had one five-year marriage and one child. She had six near-marriages, each of which ended at her instigation but not with conscious intent. As Cheryl considered her adult history, she realized it followed a pattern. When things were going well in personal relationships or at work, "something got into her" and she would "blow it." At those moments nothing mattered. She could hurt the person she loved without caring. There had been times when she came close to killing, with no thought of the consequences for herself or others. The persons with whom she shared her life were for the most part sensitive, bright, compassionate individuals who cared deeply for her. Yet she would provoke them to violence. Some have told her she could provoke to murder. She was not surprised because at those moments nothing registered; nothing mattered. Cheryl had not thought of herself as suicidal. She had had no accidents. She had had only the mildest of transitory illnesses. It did not occur to her that driving at high speed on the thruway when she had had too much to drink was suicidal. She had known well some young people who had been killed in accidents related to drinking. Somehow the reality of death had not pierced her consciousness where she herself was concerned. Stimulus-response, instinct-reaction had always been her pattern of behavior.

Cheryl's neural network design was both faulty and inadequate. In the limbic section the neural network had many loose ends. Between the limbic section and the left hemisphere there apparently were no neural connections. There was another fault. Cheryl was bright. She had talked in sentences at eight months. She had been an excellent student until age twelve. What she had learned seems not to have been translated into left hemisphere skills—logic, reason, and judgment. What she had learned had not led to a clear delineation of reality. Without firm knowledge, logic, reason, and judgment there was nothing to contribute to limbic section perception and function even if there had been a channel for that knowledge and those skills to be transmitted. The limbic section was therefore free to function without restraint according to the rules of instinct, reflex, and habit. That she had survived to age twenty-eight was a miracle.

Two Mysteries Plumbed

There are high-level performers who

> Experience no pleasure from their achievements.
> Disparage accolades and are angered by them.
> Plough ahead at a high level of proficiency plagued by doubts as to their own capability and the validity and purpose of their carefully considered efforts.

There is no objective reality to their doubts, yet they exist. They make no sense, yet they engender intense suffering and can be life threatening. In such individuals substantive, verifiable knowledge as to achievements carries no weight; logic, reason, and judgment are in abeyance. The left hemisphere is inoperative.

The right hemisphere holds sway. Ignorant of objective reality, the right hemisphere creates its own reality and musters the full force of its accumulated power to implement that reality. Its evolutionary ally, the limbic section, is in full operation in terms of dedication and commitment. Strangely, however, that dedication and commitment are not to the furtherance of right hemisphere reality. Instead, they are directed to the realization of left hemisphere values, priorities, and goals.

The miracle of commitment. The mystery of skepticism, cynicism, futility in the light of superior performance in objective reality. A nagging WHY.

A puzzle of equal complexity is the individual who is bright, knowledgeable, and even talented who can function only under supervision. Left on their own, such persons do not know where to begin. Experience has added up to nothing where know-how is concerned. If they make plans they do not follow them. If they schedule appointments, they forget them. Appointment books are of no help since such individuals do not look at them. Panic accompanies any effort: a telephone call, a scheduled or chance personal contact. These people make excellent candidates for cult groups. They may be found in the prison recidivist population. WHY? What is amiss in their personality equipment? Analysis of the phenomenon of self in terms of structure, content, and function has brought to light a number of distinguishing features that might add to our understanding and to more effective procedures for intervention and planning. The distinguishing features will be examined in two sections, "Identity Fusion" and "Identity Diffusion."

In both the case of the highly motivated, maximum-functioning individual who experiences no pleasure from achievement and of the individual who functions only under supervision in a structured program, the self is at fault. What is the fault?

Identity Fusion

Identity fusion is a complex intrapsychic phenomenon. The individual's self has progressed from the visceral, organic, experiential level to awareness that he as a person pursues his interests, develops his abilities, charts a course of action, and pursues it systematically to its goal.

There is no objective evidence that what the individual does and what he achieves have no reality for him. He does what he is expected to do and he does it to the best of his ability. No one would have any way of knowing that what he chooses to do is determined by his models of the moment. These models may range from a mechanic to a scientist to an artist. Each model presents a challenge. Each brings into play the necessary effort, energy, and capabilities for the desired goals to be achieved. The end result? The individual comes away feeling like a puppet on a string or a pawn on a chessboard, subject to the command of others.

The individual is directed by his interests and likes. His response may be purely intuitive and instinctive rather than a conscious, deliberate experience in which options are recognized and choices made. A person, a situation, a dream sets in motion something akin to an automatic pilot. The course is set and followed with no conscious control.

There has been no conscious awareness of options and choice. There has been no exercise of responsibility. There has been no recognition or acknowledgment of the individual effort that yielded the objective results. Here there lies the explanation for the individual's lack of gratification from achievement.

A curious phenomenon comes into play. Failure to recognize and acknowledge responsibility and failure to connect effort and achievement make possible a right hemisphere takeover of left hemisphere terrain—illegitimate spoils in an illegitimate war. Left hemisphere achievements are accredited to right hemisphere fantasy of omnipotence-omniscience. All we need to know and all we need to know how to do is in our brain cells. Much inherited knowledge and wisdom comes with our genes, but this is not enough for living effectively in a highly developed, technological world. This is objective reality. This is incontrovertible reality.

For the individual suffering identity fusion, the right hemisphere takeover of left hemisphere terrain carries serious risk. The right hemisphere double talks. It encourages dreams and the exercise of wings. At the same time, it is a purveyor of doom. It is phobic. Dreams assault. They dramatize in graphic images right hemisphere tragi-phobia; and often they succeed in sabotaging legitimate, hard-earned left hemisphere accomplishments.

Even as he dreams the individual may be aware that he is experiencing a dream. His left hemisphere may assure him that dreams are not predictive, and there is ample evidence to affirm this. Yet in subtle ways, like a powerful undertow, the dream invades and undermines the pursuit and the management of achievement. Bart is a graphic example.

Bart's struggle started early. At thirteen he left home and moved in with friends. There was something in the climate of his home that he found impossible to tolerate. He had to leave or he could not have survived. Bart was a bright, talented young man. His sensitivity and concern for people were readily apparent. People liked him. Throughout his life people had been available when he needed them. This became particularly clear in the college community. Professors became his friends. Bart never took advantage of their friendship. He found enrichment in it. He blossomed academically and won academic respect. An interesting phenomenon persisted throughout Bart's thirty-five-year life experience. No matter how unusual or dedicated his friends, no matter how extensive or exceptional his achievements, Bart's self-esteem remained at zero. He was nobody, nothing. The accolades he won brought him no pleasure or sense of achievement. They reflected only that others did not know how little he knew or how little he knew how to do. In believing him exceptional Bart believed, they exposed their own inadequacies. Bart was not impressed. Nothing was added to his view of himself. He saw himself as a pawn, functioning at the whim of others. Yet this was not true.

Just as Bart had left home at thirteen to escape what was for him an intolerable situation, so all his life he made the determinations that directed his life. He could have settled for being a salesman. He was a topnotch one. He could have settled for being a stockbroker. He had been eminently successful. He could have been a designer. His furniture creations had been enthusiastically received. He chose to be an architect, a difficult profession. Academic learning did not come easily. But he did go to graduate school and performed at a high level. Again, as had been true in connection with all of his endeavors, his self-assessment remained at zero. None of his achievements added up to anything. They were of no value, to no avail.

That Bart's psychological situation was a critical, possibly even life-threatening, one came to light under circumstances that defied the logic, reason, and judgment of any observer or person involved in Bart's world.

An unusual opportunity opened up for Bart. He did everything within his power to qualify for it. When he did, he experienced momentary elation and a sense of achievement. But the feeling dissipated almost as soon as it registered.

Not only did Bart question his competence. He became intensely angry at those who had certified to his capabilities. He saw himself as having been dishonest in how he had presented himself. He saw his sponsors as having been co-conspirators in his misrepresentation. At no level of relationship or experience did Bart experience trust or confidence in others as they addressed themselves to his capabilities. At no point did he have confidence in his own abilities.

There was panic and the impulse to scuttle the opportunity he had worked hard to achieve and that, according to all objective criteria, he richly deserved. What a dilemma for Bart. What a dilemma for the therapist who had supported and encouraged Bart through the years in his determination to be all that he could be.

The BONN theory of personality and behavior put Bart's dilemma into a new light. Trust became the issue around which the dilemma was clarified. If Bart could not trust himself or others, if he could not trust the objective evidence of his capabilities and his achievements, there was the possibility that Bart had no self to trust. Without a separate self there was no basis for trust or the experience of trust.

The therapist wondered: since Bart was unable to accept the assessment of others, could we establish criteria within himself that would provide an accurate base for self-judgment, a matter that was going to be of major importance in his new assignment?

A starting point was to identify the guidelines Bart had followed in achieving his success. Formalized, these might provide a base for Bart to begin to trust himself. From them might evolve clarification as to what Bart looks to others for and what criteria would be helpful in measuring the quality of the advice he is receiving. Specificity and conceptualization would serve to objectify Bart's task performance pattern and process. Logical to be sure. And with the quality of Bart's mental capability the task should pose no problems.

Fantasy. Neither Bart nor the therapist was prepared for the anger of volcanic intensity that erupted as efforts in the direction of self-rooted standards were undertaken. Bart denied any responsibility for course selection. He denied the effort and energy he had invested in his performance. He discredited both the quantity and the quality of his achievements. There was the suggestion of a complete break with reality. It was momentary.

Bart, emotionally spent, slowly regained control. Of course, it was he who had applied for the opportunity in question. Of course, it was he who had been interviewed and selected, not his mentor nor any of the many models who had contributed to his goals. He had done it. It was he who wanted to do what he had selected to do. The crisis was past. Its significance could not be dismissed. Its seriousness was great. Performance was at risk. Potential was a risk. For Bart, restriction in performance or potential placed life at risk.

A decision of mammoth proportions fell to the therapist. There were some new awarenesses and acknowledgments. Both were tentative. If one could firm them up, if one could establish beyond a doubt the fact of a separate self with its own foundation, boundaries, content, and capabilities, the highest of Bart's potentials would be within reach. There was risk in the status quo. The therapist decided to try for the stars, for intensive therapeutic intervention. She suggested a block of time. Four weeks were available when priority could be given to the therapeutic task. Bart was advised that he would need to be in as neutral and undemanding a living situation as it was possible to establish. He would need to alert his family and friends that he might have to be incommunicado for a time and that he might be difficult to be with in social functions. Bart gave serious consideration to the options available. He was puzzled by the possibility that he might be difficult to get along with, but he accepted the therapist's judgment and agreed to the program. A total of eighteen hours was required. The task was twofold:

1.   To establish the absolute—separateness: in no way and under no conditions do one or more people make one. Individuals may influence, guide, direct, and control. But it is always one separate, distinct human being acting with, for, or upon another, never as a

part of another. Incorporation, fusion, introjection—efforts to become part of another—are wishful thinking. But they cannot be. They are counter to the essential nature of the human organism.
2.   To establish beyond a doubt the connection between effort and achievement.

Establishing separateness was relatively easy. It had been under consideration in many different contexts through the whole period of treatment. What proved almost to be a Waterloo was connecting effort and achievement. What it involved for Bart was:

1.   Giving up the fantasy of omniscience—the notion that all he needed to know and all he needed to know how to do were already available in his brain.
2.   Relinquishing the certainty, the infallibility, of intuitive, inherited knowledge.
3.   Accepting acquired knowledge with all of its uncertainties and transiencies and according to it higher validity than intuitive, inherited knowledge.

By the seventeenth interview the issue was joined. There was another volcanic explosion. Bart would have liked to destroy everything in sight, especially the therapist.

The therapist was on the alert. She was worried. Was a break with reality imminent? Was the effort to replace fantasy with reality so threatening that life was at risk? Might hospitalization be necessary to weather the assault? Was the outburst a "last-ditch-stand," the crisis in the battle between left and right hemisphere control?

The therapist retreated. It was OK if Bart decided not to take the final step—wresting control from the right hemisphere and giving control to the left hemisphere. It was a major decision. Bart was a sufficiently knowledgeable, skillful, accomplished individual that he did not need to master the last rung of the psychological ladder.

We ended what had been a three-hour interview on this note. Implicit was the fact that our interview the next day would provide the direction: where to from here. Implicit also was the fact that should Bart decide to stop short of the goal, we would discuss the issues as they affected his future course of action.

A late evening telephone call brought news of victory: victory of left hemisphere control over right. Bart was clearer on the issues than he ever had been. It was as though a tremendous floodlight had illuminated the arena. Bart was sure: never had he been so sure.

The eighteenth interview confirmed the victory. Bart had slept more restfully than he had for months. Even in this brief interval since our last interview, his mind had been bounding ahead, considering all he needed to do to proceed with his new program. There was no question he wanted to do it. There was no question he could do it. If he ran into snags he would know how to arrange for help. There seemed to be no need for further therapeutic contact. Brief telephone contacts confirmed that the decision was holding, that the effects were generalizing from the professional to the personal and the social. Never in his life had Bart done anything as difficult as what we had done in these past weeks. Never had he experienced such a tremendous sense of achievement. Never had he felt so privileged or so grateful.

For the therapist the outcome was gratifying, of course. There was no question the achievement was significant and firm. What was equally clear was that intervening in identity fusion was risky. Just as the surgeon must ascertain that all physiological systems are fully functioning before he undertakes a major operation, so the therapist must make sure that the psychological systems have the basic strength and the functional capability to withstand the severing of firmly established connections. It should not be undertaken for cosmetic purposes (for example, status or wealth). It should not be undertaken if there is a choice. For Bart it had not been cosmetic. He didn't care about status and wealth. It was not elective. All his life he had been determined to be all that he could be. He could not compromise. If there was a goal within his reach, he wanted to reach it. To that end no sacrifice or personal effort was too great. Had the battle ended in defeat of the left hemisphere, Bart's survival would have been at serious risk. There had been no choice for Bart—nor for his therapist.

Identity Diffusion

Identity diffusion is the most serious of personality disorders. It was dramatized graphically by an example a taxi driver shared with me as he drove me to a radio talk show. He was a graduate student in psychology. As a part of his training he had participated in a research program on the retraining of criminal recidivists.

It was a two-year experiment. The goal was to train the prisoners in landscaping. The program went well. The men were interested, and they learned quickly and well. They became expert in their tasks. Some even displayed creative ability. All went smoothly as long as the men were supervised. Unsupervised, they did nothing. Inertia and apathy took over. Nothing interested them. They wanted to do nothing. Prior achievements carried no weight, provided no challenge.

Whether in these individuals the personucleus, the seed of self, had not grown beyond the seedling stage of early life experience or whether growth had been stunted or arrested by life trauma was not known. The evidence was clear. Whether undeveloped, stunted, or arrested, the self was virtually nonexistent.

The seedling or embryonic self is visceral. It is experienced on a purely sensory level in its most primitive stage. Hot, cold, wet, dry, comfort, discomfort, all were experienced and reacted to but without conscious awareness, without discrimination as to the nature of the experience.

Identity diffusion is to the human personality what homogenization is to milk: individual characteristics are dispersed and scattered. There is no cohesion, no core, no separateness, no identity. One young man aged twenty—bright, talented, and with dreams of saving the world—wanted to know how I knew for sure that he was real, that he was sitting in a chair in my office. How did I *know* he wasn't a figment of my imagination, just another form of space? Here was disembodiment, an extreme form of identity diffusion. Had it been more than a momentary test question, the prognosis for BONN intervention would have been very poor.

The question suggested that this individual not only lacked an identifiable self but feared the disintegration of his physical self. Not long ago he suffered severe malnutrition because he had not bothered to eat. He had given no thought to the fact that not eating could lead to death. His psychosis has been rampant for years. The BONN technique is proving effective in bringing it under control.

Where there is only a visceral self without awareness there can be no thinking or planning for oneself. A broken limb will not heal without the protection and support of a cast. A nonexistent self cannot perform without someone to lean on, someone to direct.

Conclusion

The self is central. It is the core of the executive "I." Under the psychological microscope the self appears in many forms not mutually exclusive or fixed. In one area the self may appear in tandem; in another, encapsulated; in another, surrendered; in still another, in limbo. Recognizing these variations and the contexts in which they appear is helpful in charting therapeutic procedures. Recognizing the indicators of identity fusion and identity diffusion provide boundaries to therapeutic intervention.

PART III

INTERVENTION

CHAPTER 4

Intervention:
Two Categories

BONN techniques and procedures are simple. The tasks they address are multiple, varied, and represent many levels of complexity. Hence this separate section. Corrective measures for dysfunctional patterns in neural network design were presented in Chapter II. This section on intervention will deal with dysfunctional patterns that have their origin in brain organization. The techniques and procedures have been developed in clinical practice. They are proving adaptable to the tasks of parents, educators, and individuals interested in self-development.

Intervention: Categories

Intervention within the framework of the BONN theory of personality and behavior falls into two categories:

Facilitation—the task of the parent and the educator.
Correction—the task of the therapist and the self-actualizer.

Commonalities and Differentials

Procedures

Both categories of intervention involve three steps:

> Observation.
> Assessment.
> Action.

Frame of Reference

For each category the frame of reference is the same. The BONN approach is based on the theory that *personality and behavior are preset by nature in terms of (1) sectional centrality—limbic area, right hemisphere, and left hemisphere and (2) neural network design.*

Constants

The BONN approach views as lifelong constants the four characteristics researchers have discovered in the newborn:

> The newborn does not reach out if there is nothing to reach for.
> The newborn is intrigued with the unexpected.
> The newborn loves problems as long as they are within the range of his capabilities.
> The one thing the newborn cannot and will not tolerate is boredom. When bored he withdraws and resists reinvolvement.

These four characteristics are crucial to human survival, development, and the realization of potential.

Assumptions

Common to both categories of intervention are certain basic assumptions. Among the most essential of these are the beliefs that

The human being longs for acceptance, acknowledgment, appreciation, and affection.

If behavior yields reactions other than the above, the difficulty may lie in the individual's brain organization and design, not in intent, conscious or unconscious, or in motivation, implicit or explicit. The cause may be beyond conscious awareness. It may be beyond the individual's control. The person may have no awareness or knowledge of possible alternative behaviors nor the skills to engage the options that exist.

There may be faults in the neural network design of the individual's brain—loops, short circuits, dead ends, and loose ends that interfere with perception and behavior.

Where preset brain organization places control of behavior in the archaic sections of the brain (the limbic area and the right hemisphere) behavior will be based on instinct, reflex, and habit, without consideration of reality and time or concern for consequences.

For appropriate brain management, the left hemisphere—the locus of knowledge, reason, logic, and judgment—must be in control.

For guidance the left hemisphere looks to the executive "I"—the source of values, priorities, and goals.

Crucial to the quality of the executive "I" is the quality of the "self."

Absolutes

In addition to these assumptions, undergirding the BONN frame of reference are the following concepts:

All elements in nature, including the human personality, are in a constant state of flux.

There is exquisite order in nature's infinite variety.

Laws govern nature's order and diversity: biological laws govern the body and aid the physician; laws of aerodynamics govern flight and aid the pilot; laws of psychodynamics govern the mind and can aid the parent, educator, therapist, and self-actualizer.

The human mind is intrigued with the laws of nature as they apply to the vast variety of living organisms. It is amazing what we know about bacteria, fish, reptiles, and birds, and we marvel at their diversity. But where the human personality is concerned, diversity is viewed as deviance or pathology. Differences in sexual preference or in life style elicit dismay and disparagement. There is none of the fascination that is elicited by the diversity in other species. The reason is that studying oneself is perhaps the most difficult of all tasks. That is what the brain is expected to do when we examine human personality and behavior. That is what the brain is being expected to do when we consider how the brain is organized, how its neural network is designed, and how this organization and design affect behavior.

In the light of the inherent complexity of the task, it is amazing that some very simple procedures can effect major changes in perceptions, feelings, and behavior that generalize and are firm.

Requirements

Whether the task is developmental or correctional, the requirements are the same:

Practice until the desired behavior is established.

Continuing development of left hemisphere knowledge and skills

Vigilance to ensure that left hemisphere knowledge is being used to keep archaic interference under control.

Assessment of neural network adequacy to ensure channeling of left hemisphere realities to the offending areas.

Erratic, sporadic use of the procedures is an alert. It may suggest inadequate understanding of the importance of practice. It may be a clue to faults in the self. Erratic, sporadic use of the procedures calls for an overall review of accomplishments in the light of whether the accomplishments are to the individual's liking. It calls for a reassessment of commitment, goals, risks, and options.

CHAPTER 5

Techniques: Sectional Interference

Wide-eyed wonder, disbelief, and intrigue register visibly the moment one begins to talk about an individual's problems in terms of brain organization and design. Eyes languid on arrival light up. Limp posture reflecting discouragement becomes erect. Often the end-of-the-spine slouch shifts to an edge-of-the-chair perch.

Frame of Reference

Every individual is born with an individually organized and designed brain.

The organization and design are determined by nature. Sometimes the pattern is similar to that of one's ancestors. Sometimes it is different from anything anyone in the family has known or heard about. Nature reserves the right to invent. Never satisfied, sometimes nature's inventions are trial-and-error experiments. Nature is always striving to create something better. We know this from the mutants, the "sports" that are found among every living organism in nature.

There is noticeable relief as the individual hears this explanation—sometimes a deep breath, shoulders suddenly relaxed, and a slow, thoughtful, hesitant smile: "You mean it's nobody's fault.

There is nothing wrong?'' There follows invariably the recounting of confusions and worries.

> As far back as Cher could remember people said she was "bad." She didn't know why. She didn't know what she did that made them say it. She certainly did not intend to be "bad." She wanted more than anything else to be loved. She needed love to survive, and she took it wherever she could find it, often with disastrous results. She knew she did things over and over again that made people angry. She said and did things that were hurtful. She didn't mean to. She just knew no other way.

Modifiability

We have learned from the cults that the brain, no matter how well endowed genetically or how well nurtured educationally, can be dismantled. Its genetic capability can be immobilized and its knowledge become encapsulated, unavailable for use. The personality can be divested of the capacity for joy, desire, pain, anticipation. Thinking as an experience can be destroyed. Imagination as a lure to living can be rendered inoperative. The brain surrenders to the most primitive arena of mental experience, the limbic section, where the "promise of the womb" is fulfilled as nearly as is possible within the context of life in the world.

The cult offers the promise of unqualified individual love in the bosom of the group. The success of the spider-to-the-fly technique, the on-the-spot assurance of "love," attests to the brain's vulnerability to the lure, the eternal search for the womb. It is evidence, too, of the tremendous power of the law of gravity or inertia—the universal wish to obtain the greatest return for the least expenditure of energy.

The kind of programming and repetitive techniques used so effectively by the cults to dismantle the brain can be used to reorganize and redesign the brain in the interest of self-realization. Conscious determination and commitment to left hemisphere control are the essentials. There are three steps to bringing the limbic section and the right hemisphere under the control of the left hemisphere:

1. One must be aware of limbic section or right hemisphere intrusion.

2. The left hemisphere must stop the intrusion with "not now, perhaps later."

3. If the archaic sections do not listen, one must stop what one is doing and do something else. The brain can concentrate on only one thing at a time. Changing focus halts the flow of energy.

If these procedures are followed consistently, the neural channels carrying the offending stimuli will atrophy as do muscles when they are unused.

Resistance

Human beings for the most part do not take kindly or eagerly to the idea of change. They prefer what comes naturally, without effort. They cling to the familiar, the known. Resistance to change comes in many forms, sometimes overtly, clearly, sometimes subtly, as an undercurrent.

The "I'm Not Interested"

Roy wanted to ensure that I understood he had come under protest. His aunt had given him $25 to keep the appointment. He needed the money. Protest registered in every part of his sixteen-year-old being. His eyes flashed in anger. He slouched in his chair as though trying to be invisible. Roy did not know why his family was so insistent that he talk with me.

He was content with the way his life was going. He enjoyed being the dictator at home with his mother and sister cowering at his demands. He wasn't doing any differently than his father. True. The difference was that his father was an adult and the head of the household. Roy was a child. He carried no authority. He did not have the right to threaten his mother or his sister with physical violence under any circumstances. (I made clear I did not believe anyone had that right.) Roy had no right to tease his sister until she cried. He had no right to order her off the phone. Only his parents had that right. Roy disagreed violently. There were no limits to his rights. The family would have to learn to respect them. Roy did not believe that his parents would refuse to have him live in the family if his behavior continued as it was.

Although Roy's perception of reality was inaccurate and his sense of right and wrong tenuous, there seemed to be enough connection with reality that I considered it worthwhile to explain to him the organization of the brain and the fact that the limbic section and the right hemisphere of his brain were in collusion, distorting the realities of family living. Roy listened restively. What I was saying was ridiculous. He had no intention of changing. He had no intention of seeing me again. I recommended to the family that if Roy's out-of-control behavior continued they consider hospitalization.

A break with reality seemed imminent if not already in effect, and his aggressive impulses posed real danger to both his mother and sister. I was relieved that Roy was not driving. He had described vividly how if anything were in his path—person, or car—he would have to make a conscious decision as to whether he would stop or plough ahead.

Three months later Roy's mother came in again to discuss the recurring problem with her husband. She made no mention of Roy. When I asked, she said: "Oh, he's fine!" He and his sister are the best of friends. They enjoy each other's company and spend many hours playing games together. In general, Roy is cooperative, doing his chores without having to be reminded. He continues to do well in school. One interview and a psychosis was under control. It was no miracle. Right hemisphere and limbic interference had come under the control of left hemisphere knowledge, logic, reason, judgment, and reality. Being able to continue to live in the family was sufficiently important to Roy that change was undertaken.

The "I Haven't Decided"

With Harold resistance took another form. He had been intrigued, and excited in the first interview when I explained how his right hemisphere was interfering with his learning. In the six years Harold had been in school he had never done an assignment. He had never turned in a paper. His teacher had suggested that his parents bring him to see me because she was worried that a break with reality might be imminent. Harold had agreed enthusiastically to a second appointment. I had explained the three-step procedure he could use to keep the right hemisphere under control.

Harold came to the second appointment, but there was a marked difference in his demeanor. His hair was disheveled, his clothes in disarray. He sat dejected, with his eyes fixed to the floor. Under his breath he said, almost inaudibly: "I haven't decided." I knew what he meant. I assured Harold it was OK. He and I knew he was extremely bright (I had had ample evidence of that in our first discussion). Anytime Harold decided he wanted to learn he would be able to do so. He didn't have to do it now.

Harold's mother was waiting in the lobby. I suggested that Harold have her talk with me while he waited in the lobby. I explained the problem to Mrs. K. Harold was extremely bright. It was possible that the public school system was not the right place for him. Mrs. K. was incredulous. She looked at me as though I had come from outer space. "How could I say that? "Harold can't do the simplest of chores," she said.

When Mrs. K. came in a week later she had an amazing report. After Harold's last appointment with me he had gone to his teacher and asserted: "I want to be a 'B' student." He paid up his class dues and became actively involved for the first time in the class project. One interview. No miracle. Instead, Harold, in charge of how his brain functioned, had made a decision. He proceeded immediately to implement it.

The "I Don't Want To"

Rodney expressed his resistance in another way. He was not undecided, as Harold had been. He was definite. He had used the three-step procedure for one week. It had worked. With no special effort he could keep his right hemisphere from interfering with left hemisphere learning. He didn't want to. He enjoyed his daydreams. He wasn't about to give up the privilege of daydreaming whenever he wanted to. That was a decision I indicated Rodney was free to make. There was no point in his seeing me again. I wondered, however, whether Rodney would be willing to come in for one interview at the end of the semester so that I could know how things were going. He agreed willingly.

When the time came for his appointment, Rodney informed his parents that he didn't want to see me. That was OK. His mother would come instead. Her report was as dramatic as Harold's mother's had been. Rodney had become a "B" student. His behavior at home was appropriate for a twelve-year-old. He did his chores, and he was cooperative in family activities. He entered freely into family discussions. The family was delighted with the changes.

The "What About the Risks?"

Resistance took still another form with Mr. L. Mr. L. had tried the three-step procedure for a week. There was no question, it worked. It worked easily, without effort. All Mr. L. had to do was say "Concentrate," and the left hemisphere kept the right hemisphere under control. Mr. L. had two questions: How did I know he wouldn't suffer a heart attack from day-to-day stress if he didn't escape into fantasy? And what would he do for fun? I could not assure Mr. L. that he wouldn't have a heart attack. I could have no way of knowing that. As for fun, I suggested that Mr. L., with his many talents, could find fun in reality as well as in fantasy. We had reached a crossroad. Mr. L. had a choice. He could continue "as is." If he did, there was little likelihood that his marriage would survive—and that his marriage was in serious jeopardy had been clear from the outset. If Mr. L. decided to engage change, there would be risks. Mr. L. was very thoughtful. He made a decision. He wanted to correct whatever it was that was threatening his marriage. He did.

The "My Mind Left the Room"

The most touching kind of resistances occurred with twenty-nine-year-old Winthrop, who had a master's degree in sociology. The only job he had been able to hold was in a haberdashery shop owned by a relative. He hated the work. He wanted only to paint and spent every free hour at his easel. Winthrop did not know why his parents insisted he see me. They had given him a choice: he could see me or he could find another place to live. His attitude, his behavior, his need for isolation were more than they could bear. Their marriage was in jeopardy. Both his mother and his father assured him of their love and concern. But they were not willing to put themselves at risk. Winthrop had come.

At some point during each session he reminded me that he had come under duress. He wished that what I said made more sense to him than it did. He wished he had more confidence in me. It was OK, I assured him. I had confidence in what I was doing with him. As long as he came and tried to understand what I was saying, I was willing to see him.

During the fifteenth hour, the first week that his parents were away on a three-week vacation, a blankness clouded Winthrop's face as I began to talk with him. At his request, I started to clarify for him what he would have to do to bring under control his worries about aggressive impulses as the possibility of success loomed on the horizon. He wanted very much to be a successful painter. Indeed, his talent had been affirmed by many people. Yet his paintings had always fallen short of expectations. Winthrop didn't want worries about out-of-control behavior to block his way if he could avoid it in any way.

There was a way, but it would take conscious effort. Winthrop had to make an all-out commitment to have the left hemisphere in control. For him this meant wresting control from his powerful limbic section.

To wrest control from the limbic section the strengths of the left hemisphere—logic, reason, and judgment—would have to be carefully developed. The left hemisphere would have to keep sharply aware of reality and time. Like the rock of Gibraltar, the left hemisphere with its knowledge and skills must be indomitable. Only then would it be able to keep within bounds the unreasoning, aggressive impulses of Winthrop's limbic area.

Aware of the blankness that had taken over, I asked Winthrop if he had any reaction to what I had said. (Usually people begin to yawn uncontrollably as they listen to such explanations. Such a response is an indicator of limbic protest.) Winston exhibited no such reaction. I wondered if he had listened or heard. His response was sober, his facial expression puzzled. His "mind had left the room," he stated simply. Could he tell me when this had happened? He couldn't. I wasn't surprised. I was pretty sure he had tuned out when I began to explain what would be necessary if he was to be free of worry about his aggressive impulses. I had pointed out that he would have to be able to assert firmly, without a shadow of doubt, that whatever he did would have to be related to reality, using the best of his knowledge, logic, reason, judgment. The limbic area of his brain had heard me. It realized, I explained, that its authority and power were in jeopardy. It succeeded in cutting off the channel from the limbic section to the left hemisphere. Winthrop's rational, logical mind stopped functioning. From this we both had an indication of the difficult task that faced us.

Winthrop asked a searching, perceptive question: Where was his "I"—that part of him that was supposed to be in control?

In the few weeks that Winston and I met we had not reached the point where I felt it was appropriate to consider the issue of "self." I suggested that perhaps in our next interview we could pursue the self-inventory Winston was supposed to have worked on. Then we might begin to determine the state of his "self" and to consider why it had not been able to prevent take-over by the limbic section, such as Winthrop had just experienced.

Two broken appointments were the aftermath of this session. Had we reached a crossroad? Was it the end of the line? Winthrop's parents would be back in a week and a half. Would their return bring Winthrop back? The day of his second missed appointment Winthrop telephoned. Could he see me later that day? I could not arrange that. Would his next regular appointment be OK? It would. How was he doing, I asked. He had no complaints. He sounded fine.

Winthrop arrived early as usual. In the two weeks since he had seen me he had done some exciting things with his painting. His job, the first he had had in years with someone other than a relative, was going well. He had been at it six weeks and he had no complaints.

Winthrop was not looking forward to his parents' return. He wished he could afford his own apartment. But he could literally do so only at a poverty level. I did not encourage him to pursue this direction. His parents were able and willing to help him. What he was trying to do with me was important and should have priority.

Winthrop had a question: What could one do with a person who didn't want to change? I explained that I believed every individual has a right to live his life as he chooses, assuming, of course, that his rights do not impinge on the rights of others. Winthrop smiled as I gave the example: "My freedom ends with your nose." I also knew from long experience that the one thing the human organism resists vehemently is the "must." In general, it defies the "must." Taking these two issues into account, what I do is spell out the options available to the individual, as well as the costs and risks of each option. The individual then makes a choice.

We picked up the subject of "self," which had been touched on in our previous interview. For the first time I traced for Winthrop the steps from seedling to full-blown self. Winthrop thought he was aware and was moving toward acknowledging himself. He had not yet reached the stage of appraisal and was inclined to question whether anyone could appraise himself. I assured him it was possible and necessary if one was to be autonomous and authentic. To be able to appraise oneself one had to be clear on values, priorities, and goals so that one could truly respond to: "Will the real me please stand up?" Here was something Winthrop wanted to explore fully. He realized it would have to wait.

Winthrop wanted to go on for a second hour. We moved into the area of the "faulty self." Granted that Winthrop was well on the way to having a self, did he fit into any of the four categories of faulty self? He thought he could put himself into each of the four categories at one time or another. He could not settle for any dominant one. I shared with him my assessment. Winthrop belonged in the encapsulated category. He considered the characteristics of this category seriously and did not quarrel with my assessment. But he was troubled. He believed a certain amount of encapsulation was necessary for him to become an artist with individual distinction. If that was the case, I indicated that then, of course, he could not afford to change that part of his personality. He would not want to jeopardize what was essential to his goal. Winthrop became thoughtful. It seemed to him that there were areas in which encapsulation was a deterrent to his progress as an artist. This was what he wanted to change.

We had reached a milestone. I wanted to ensure that Winthrop and I were together on its significance. For the first time Winthrop was acknowledging that there was something about himself he wanted to change. He would no longer be coming to our sessions because of his parents' insistence, he said. Here was a turning point in treatment.

We have seen that resistances fade away in the presence of choice. Resistances may also convert to commitment as evidence accumulates that the brain can be brought into harmony through the exercise of simple procedures.

Energy Deployment: The Basic Laws of Nature

Mothers attest to the differences in children even in embryo. Some are placid, easy to carry. Others are restive, as though impatient with their constricting environment, eager to be free. One may assume legitimately that the prevailing law of nature is preset, as is body structure, facial features, and skin coloring. As one thinks of intervention it is well to consider whether the individual will welcome change (the law of magnetism) or resist it (the law of gravity or inertia and the law of conservation). For clinicians this factor may well be not only a determinant of case selection but of therapeutic procedure. Certainly it is a factor that needs to be taken into account in goal delineation.

Marshall was an engineer who had been unemployed for two years. For months he wondered whether he would ever break out of the economic doldrums, whether he would ever realize his professional ambitions. His resources were almost exhausted, and he had to do something. A friend had recommended that he see me. Marshall was deeply committed to yoga, finding it relaxing and comforting. He had also read up on meditation. He brought me books and tapes so that I might understand his urgent search for peace and tranquillity.

Marshall wanted very much to marry and have children. The woman with whom he was living was good to be with, understanding, patient, and nondemanding. Yet she did not measure up to his dream or to his family's expectations. He liked sharing his home with her but not his social life.

I explained to Marshall why I would not read the books or listen to the tapes. For me to get into his world would not be helpful for him. The issue that had to be addressed was whether Marshall really wanted to change. Or did he want only to design his life so that it more effectively satisfied his needs and wants?

A week's experimentation with a BONN procedure (a two-hour, random library exploration) provided the answer. Marshall wanted only more of what he already had. He wanted desperately to have me come into his world.

I explained again why this was not possible, why it would not be helpful. It seemed to me that at this point in Marshall's life the BONN technique was not appropriate for him. The BONN technique focused on the realization of individual potential. The one thing it could not guarantee was the peace and tranquillity that Marshall seemed to want so badly.

Should Marshall's wants change, should he be more interested in developing his mind and his many talents, the BONN technique would certainly be helpful to him. Marshall has not returned. Instead, he has gone back to his first job. This opportunity had always been available to him. He had resisted the return for twelve years.

In the natural sciences we have managed the law of gravity so that we were able to reach the moon. There is no doubt that the same feat can be realized with the human personality. Dissatisfaction with the status quo has to be intense. Determination to expand and enhance the life experience must be without qualification or reservation. Essential to maximizing life's potential are the following ingredients:

Clarity as to one's innate and potential capabilities.
Clarity as to one's interests and preferences.
Models to help one find the "stars."
Mentors to help one chart the course.

The Process of Change

Over a period of five months (from December 1978 to April 1979) I became aware of the dramatic effectiveness of the BONN procedure and technique. For example, in one case, Hester's, archaic worries of aggression that had eluded six months of traditional therapy were brought under control. In this period of time treatment ended, for Hester had achieved her goal: a position for which she was highly qualified and which she had been trying for a year to make herself apply for. At this writing, three years later, the gains hold.

Marlene's situation posed a dilemma:

Marlene and I had been working together for about a year. Only once in that period did she venture out of her feeling of lethargy and futility to consider what she might do with her life. When I explained the new BONN procedure to Marlene she became troubled. She claimed she wouldn't be able to use the new procedure because she was never aware of when her right hemisphere intruded or took over. If that was true, what we would have to do,

I explained, was to develop her abilities of self-observation and self-awareness.

When Marlene came in the next week, she was exuberant. Not only had she begun to be aware of the activity of her right hemisphere, but she had remembered some crucial experiences in her life that she had completely forgotten. In these new-found memories lay a possible explanation for her apathy, her cynicism, and her marginal performance in school and in work.

For the first time in her twenty-five years Marlene felt she was in control of her life. She had made some new friends. She was learning how to ski. She had joined a dance group. Even more, she was beginning to consider work that might pose more of a challenge to her.

Five months after Marlene was introduced to the new procedure, she found herself running a department in which she had been employed in lesser capacities for about a year and a half. She was in charge of purchasing, staff development, and staff management. Her new responsibilities were challenging, and she enjoyed them. For the first time Marlene looked forward to learning.

Using the neural network procedures, Bill was able after twelve interviews to set aside his archaic fantasies of omnipotence, magical power, and rivalry with his father that had plagued him for most of his twenty-five years. (For these dysfunctions he had had traditional treatment for about a year.) His chronic abdominal distress was gradually dissipating, even though the externals in his life situation were still marked by the unknown. He had begun to know for the first time the satisfaction that comes with being a disciplined and responsible adult. Finally, too, he was experiencing the relief of being able to accord and benefit by the knowledge and expertise of his seniors. Most impressive of all, Bill was able to allow himself the pleasure of being a learner. What a relief it was not to be burdened by having to know it all. How exciting it was to consider what more there was to learn and master as life went on.

Jennifer, after just one application of the three-step procedure, found that for the first time in her life her mind was at rest. She was comfortable with who and what she was. The energy that was suddenly available to her was phenomenal in quantity and quality. She was able to do a wide variety of things, and with energy to spare. Never had she experienced such feelings. Of course, she was afraid to trust it, afraid it wouldn't last. There were endless things she wanted to attempt. Finally, she was convinced that she had the capability to do whatever she decided she wanted to do.

But it was ten-year-old Debra who gave me the most graphic, dramatic description of the effectiveness of the BONN procedures. Debra's mother had wanted me to see her daughter for four years. I had always considered under-twelve-year-olds beyond the range of my expertise. In addition, over the years I had had ample evidence that Debra's problems could be managed through parental guidance. Suddenly, a year and half ago, with a divorce and a major housing move pending, Debra's problems took on an urgency that I believed required direct intervention. I decided to see Debra, to her mother's delight. We had five sessions. We discussed how childhood fantasies were affecting Debra's relationships with her younger brother and with her friends. Five interviews seemed to be all Debra needed. Things went better at home and with her relationships. She no longer had to take quantities of candy to school every day to distribute among her friends. She made the move to the new neighborhood and the new school without incident. She made new friends, without the aid of candy.

A year and a half later (in January 1979) Debra called me. She was having trouble falling asleep, and her dreams were scary.

Debra made sure that her mother would be waiting for her downstairs instead of in the waiting room, which is not soundproof. She then proceeded to bring me up-to-date. A more complete review of what had happened since we last met would be difficult to imagine. She touched on all areas that had given her concern. When she finished, I told her I had learned some things since I had seen her last that I would like to tell her about. I started to tell her about the left and right hemispheres of the brain. She stopped me. She knew all about that. Her mother had told her. I then proceeded to apply this brain concept to the problems of sleeping and bad dreams that Debra was experiencing. Debra was her usual attentive self, asking for clarification as she found it necessary.

When she came in a week later, she told me she was better. Getting to sleep was not so difficult, and her dreams were not so scary. But, said Debra defiantly, "I don't want to give up what's in the right hemisphere of my brain. I am in a creative writing class and I don't want to give that up." I assured her we weren't going to do anything to interfere with the creative part of her right hemisphere. All we wanted to do was to stop the right hemisphere from doing the things that interfered with what the left hemisphere wanted to do. Mused Debra: "You mean the two sides of my brain should be friends?" Yes, indeed.

Debra chattered on for a few moments, and then confided that her teacher had scolded her because she had been talking in class instead of listening. "That was the right side of my brain," Debra explained in a whisper. I was curious. I wondered what would happen if Debra did not allow the right side of her brain to do that. Debra's face clouded. Words tumbled. I had never before known Debra to stutter. She took a deep breath and stated soberly: "I would be very smart. I would be very smart in math and literature."

"And what would be wrong with that?" I asked. Without hesitating, Debra asserted: "My friends would hate me." I had to concur. That might very well happen.

Psychologist Alvin Mahrer points out that if one becomes a self-actualizer, one is likely to become a persona non grata among one's friends and relatives. I believed it was important for Debra to know that what she said was true. That was one of the risks. But I thought she and I could figure out a way that Debra could excel in school and still have friends.

Debra told her father she was seeing me. He was livid. He did not want me to meddle in his daughter's life. He ordered Debra not to see me. He threatened me with court action. Debra in the next interview was worried. I reassured her. I would deal with whatever her father did. She would not have to come in again. Debra knew all she needed to know to manage her brain so that it did what she wanted it to do. Should she run into difficulty, she could tell her mother. Her mother and I would figure out how to help her. At this writing, four years later, I have not seen Debra professionally again. However, I was invited to join in the celebration of her fourteenth birthday and to see her perform in school plays. She is an outstanding student, a cheerleader, and a leader among her peers in all areas.

The changes in Debra became apparent immediately. One month after my last session with her, her mother attended the regular school conference. The teachers' reports were glowing. Not only had Debra's academic performance sky-rocketed but her relationships with her friends had taken on a dimension they had never had before. Everyone wanted to know from Debra's mother what accounted for all of these changes.

It was from Friedrich that I learned what a difficult task it was to "convert" from right to left hemisphere dominance.

Friedrich had spent eight of his sixteen years in a treatment insti-
tution. He was charged with delinquency when he left the treatment institution without permission. He sold a stamp collection he had inherited and thumbed his way to the West Coast. His plan was to stow away on a freighter to India and become a student of Indian philosophy. His aim ultimately was to become a guru. When no freighter to India was available, Friedrich considered building a raft and sailing on alone. What did he know about building a raft or navigating a raft across an ocean? Nothing. Did he have money for food? No. How suicidal was he? Very. Here were monosyllabic answers to crucial questions—enough to indicate that Friedrich had some awareness of reality. What had made Friedrich decide to call his father for funds to return home? He had realized one night, as he burrowed into a ravine to sleep, that the only people who cared about him and the only people he cared about were the people in his home town. He decided to return. Here was further evidence of reality connection.

Friedrich's behavior upon his return was bizarre. He stood spread-
eagle, naked against the wall for hours, humming in monotone and swaying to his self-designed rhythm. He spent hours in the shower. He stared glassily into space unaware of what was going on about him, unresponsive to his father's efforts to engage him in conver-
sation. The treatment institution recommended that he be placed in the detention home in relation to his runaway syndrome, or that he be placed in a mental hospital. They believed that their program had nothing more to offer him.

Friedrich's father had benefited dramatically from the neural net-
work approach that I used. He asked me to see Friedrich. I agreed. A tall, lithe, handsome young man arrived with his father and slouched

sullenly in the chair. His father explained why he had asked me to see him. It was evident immediately that Friedrich would be able to talk with me. There was no reason for his father to stay. As soon as Mr. A. left Friedrich sat on the floor, took off his shoes, and with hands together in prayerlike fashion answered the questions indicated above. I explained to Friedrich what I had learned from recent brain research about the three sections of the brain and how they affected behavior. It seemed to me that Friedrich's behavior was being directed and controlled by his right hemisphere without regard for reality and therefore he was having trouble. Friedrich listened intently. From what I had said about the right hemisphere he was sure I was right. But he wasn't sure he wanted things otherwise. That I pointed out was a crucial question. Only if he wanted things to be different was there any point to our talking. He wasn't sure but he would like to try. He would come in again.

Two days later Friedrich came in. The report from his father in between indicated that Friedrich's time sense was poor. His judgment was poor. He had almost started a fire while cooking. He had wanted to go to the lobby of the apartment inappropriately dressed.

Friedrich indicated that he had been thinking about our discussion the other day. He wondered what he could do to take control away from the right hemisphere. I asked him whether he was aware of when the right hemisphere invaded reality. Sometimes he was aware of this invasion. Not always, and not always immediately. That was the first step, I explained: to be aware. The second step was to stop the invasion. If the right hemisphere did not stop on the instruction of the left hemisphere—"that's not right"; "we won't do that now. Maybe later." Friedrich was to stop what he was doing and do something else. I explained the principle of this.

The brain could concentrate on only one thing at a time. Stopping and doing something else stopped the flow of energy from the right hemisphere and gave the left hemisphere with its focus on reality an opportunity to take control. Friedrich listened. He was obviously intrigued, but almost equally skeptical. As he sat on the floor in meditation fashion he was tempted to dismiss what I had been saying as a "cult." What confused him was that I didn't seem to have a following and didn't seem interested in developing one.

By the fourth interview Friedrich was definite and clear. He wanted me to know he had not made a firm decision to do it my way, but he would try. He had made one decision. He wanted to go back to school. I thought that was fine. I suggested he take only a partial program and only subjects he could enjoy. My thinking was (and I shared it with him) that he had been through a very taxing month on his West Coast jaunt. He undoubtedly was physically and psychologically exhausted. It was important that he not overtax either his physical or psychological system. Friedrich disagreed vehemently. He would not take a partial program. He would go to all of his classes, full time.

The next day he was at all of his classes. In the year that has passed Friedrich has missed one or two days of school, and that was due to illness. The level of his performance has fluctuated, sometimes superlative, sometimes failing. Over the summer he took three remedial courses at a community college. His high school teacher at the end of the summer reported that in her wildest dreams she would never have imagined the level of Friedrich's summer achievement. Friedrich's determination has bordered on compulsion. He wanted not only to eliminate any gap that had been created by his institutional experience, but he also wanted to be able to do what the most accomplished students were able to do, especially in math.

He was reading extensively: for example, philosophy and the autobiographies of Albert Einstein and Buckminster Fuller. The pressure he was placing on his psychological system was cause for worry. Friedrich had to be reminded over and over again that he was only sixteen. There were many years for him to acquire the knowledge and the skills that he would need to have to be the scientist he wanted to be. If he continued to put himself under such pressures his brain might go on strike. Such a response would only reinforce the strength of the right hemisphere. Friedrich's experience following his summer courses gave him evidence of the risk I had been alerting him to. He had been able to maintain left hemisphere control, but only with great effort. It was hard work. The only thing that held him on course was the realization that unless he was able to do it life would not be worth living.

He likened the dilemma to that of countries that had to defend their borders against enemies who were in constant readiness to invade. He found that if he wasn't on the alert, if he allowed his defending forces to weaken, right hemisphere invasion was certain to occur. It was powerful, subtle, and persistent in its intrusions. Friedrich had identified the conditions that weakened the defensive forces:

1. Physical fatigue.
2. Feeling sorry for himself.

3. Lamenting the years he had spent in placement.

4. Listening to the wrong kind of music.

5. Seeing one's old friends. Even new friends seemed quickly to fall into the category of old friends. It wasn't easy to find the kinds of people that nurtured and gave support to the new self Friedrich was trying to develop.

Friedrich wondered if these conditions would always be true. It seemed to me that Friedrich needed to look upon his condition much as one looks upon an allergy. Given certain conditions, the allergy is activated. People with physical allergies know what foods to avoid. People with psychological allergies need to know what experiences to avoid. Friedrich's analysis should serve him in good stead, and Friedrich was certain that it would. There were times, however, when this young man wanted to check out whether he could go right hemisphere. He could, but it was not easily done. It felt as though the neural network had really begun to atrophy.

There was still some ambivalence. Friedrich wasn't sure he wanted to relinquish choice completely. I acknowledged that this was a decision that only Friedrich could make. He knew how to keep the right hemisphere under control. He knew how to reinforce control of the left hemisphere. The choice would always be his. Even if certain neural networks should atrophy, there is the possibility that the brain with its phenomenal potential could either reconstruct the atrophied strands or create new ones to bring about the results the individual intended. Friedrich remembered clearly when at age six he relinquished control to the right hemisphere. There was a time when he had a choice. Then at one point choice was no longer his and he became prisoner of his right hemisphere.

The fact that Friedrich has two psychotic siblings older than himself reinforced Friedrich's worry. Right hemisphere dominance apparently was a family characteristic. He realized that this made the task of consolidating left hemisphere control especially critical for him. Friedrich was sure his commitment and determination would hold, and that once his brain was reorganized to left hemisphere centrality he would not have to worry about psychosis.

Two weeks short of a year Friedrich announced thoughtfully, soberly, that he still had problems but that they were within the normal range. He did not need to see me anymore. We reviewed what we had achieved in the seventy-eight hours of counseling.

What had remained untouched was the area of relationships. Friedrich believed it was more important that he consolidate his left hemisphere achievements and move on with his education before tackling relationships—or, indeed, his limbic section.

A year has passed. I have not seen Friedrich. I have learned from his family that he completed high school with honors. He worked all summer and saved enough money to travel in Europe on his own for three months. Currently he is in a training program in a sophisticated scientific field. Friedrich believes this program will help him to pursue his education in science at some future date. His current program makes it possible for him to be self-supporting and ensures him a bonus that he will be able to use to further his education.

In reminiscing with his family about his experiences with me, Friedrich marveled that two interviews based on the BONN theory had brought his psychosis under control. What a contrast to seven years of various types of therapy while he was in a treatment institution. Friedrich was convinced the BONN theory was something very special.

Sectional interferences manifest themselves in a number of other ways. From the right hemisphere come forebodings of disaster in dreams, primarily as success or fulfillment seems in the offing. From the limbic area come:

Hunger pangs even though one has had sufficient food.

Fatigue when one has had ample rest.

Respiratory discomfort with no apparent physical cause.

If these tendencies develop into chronic patterns one may suspect inadequate channels connecting the limbic section and the left hemisphere. The realities known to the left hemisphere have no avenue for reaching the limbic section. The limbic section is free to function autonomously and autocratically without regard for knowledge, logic, reason, or judgment. It does so often in its own sectional interest rather than in the interest of the individual as a whole.

Network Insufficiency Correction

Should this be the case, the task of the individual is to develop
more adequate neural connections between the left hemisphere
and the limbic section. This can be done with a simple procedure,
but it is a procedure that must be repeated over and over again
until there is evidence that the limbic section and the left hemisphere are in communication. It is like digging a tunnel through
a mountain. One whittles away at the obstruction. The instrument
is a statement of the facts:

> Eating is for nutrition. Nothing else.
> Fatigue is for lack of energy. Nothing else.
> Breathing difficulty is organic. Nothing else.

Should the limbic section continue to ignore the facts after they
have been sufficiently practiced, the limbic must be taken to task:
it has no right to usurp the powers of the autonomic systems to
serve its nationalistic, sectional interest. The autonomic systems
belong to the personality as a whole and should serve the best
interest of the individual. It is not in the best interest of the individual to experience ravenous hunger the moment he settles
down to study calculus. It is not in the best interest of the individual
that he experience exhaustion when approaching preparation for
an examination. It is not in the best interest of the individual that
he experience difficulty breathing as soon as he sits down to write
a paper. These are limbic section interferences with left hemisphere activity. They represent the limbic section's interference
with left hemisphere goals.

Where the right hemisphere intrudes with its archaic phobias
there is nothing one can do except ignore it. Right hemisphere
content is not alterable. It is a waste of time to try to convince
the right hemisphere of its irrationality. The limbic section learns.
Its reactions can be upgraded. Its responses can be brought into
harmony with reality. The right hemisphere does not learn. It
does not concern itself with consensus reality. It creates its own
reality and is preoccupied with it. Controlling right hemisphere

irrationality from invading and disrupting left hemisphere activity and goals is our only recourse with our current level of knowledge and skill.

Summary

Sectional interference can affect rationality and divest the total organism of energy. It can erect roadblocks in the way of life planning and self-realization. The archaic, instinct-controlled sections of the brain, especially if they are in collusion, can bring to a halt the best of well-laid plans.

In tow, under the direction of a well-equipped left hemisphere and a fully developed executive "I," these sections with their vast store of inherited wisdom and individual skills can contribute breadth and depth. They can offer both anchorage and wings to the individual's life experience, as well as the opportunity for the person to maximize the capabilities with which he has been endowed.

CHAPTER 6

Techniques:
Self/Others/Situation

"With artificial light we lengthen the day. With man-made lenses we see the stars and into living cells. With cameras we extend vision through time and space, witnessing what we were not there to see. By artifice, we enhance our understanding of the world and our place in it."[4] In similar vein the BONN approach, like a giant floodlight, illuminates aspects of personality and behavior not clearly seen before.

The Task

Chapter V, which dealt with techniques for dealing with sectional interferences, centered on three major issues:

Commitment to left hemisphere control of brain activity.

Procedures for establishing and maintaining left hemisphere control.

Equipping the left hemisphere with the knowledge and skills it requires to establish and maintain control over the limbic section and the right hemisphere.

The techniques are simple and explicit. The same is true for the techniques required for dealing with problems of self/others/situation. Yet there is a difference in the scope of intervention.

> *Self* involves issues of *structure*—is the self fully established and whole—and issues of *function*—is the individual functioning appropriately according to the demands of reality?
>
> *Other* involves the issue of separateness—does the individual realize that he and others are separate and distinct?
>
> *Situation* involves issues of reality—is the individual fully aware of reality, its possibilities and its limitations, where people, things, and experiences are concerned?

The most dramatic finding of the BONN approach is the pervasiveness of the self without a firmly developed core. Much of this chapter will be devoted to the examination of this phenomenon in its many guises and to the procedures that have proved effective.

The Self: Structure/Function

A blueprint of the self is produced at conception. In seedling state the self is without form. It is a potential, not a product. Its behavior is random, without plan or purpose. Its reactions are visceral, sensory, and without awareness. Between the seedling and the full-blown self is a four-dimensional span.

> Awareness—being conscious of being.
>
> Acknowledgment—recognizing the consciousness as belonging to oneself.
>
> Assessment—considering the significance of the experience to self and others
>
> Action—making a decision as to response.

The most obvious trait of the seedling self is randomness. There is no cause–effect connection or any sense of participation, involvement, or responsibility. Behavior is not only random but automatic, that is, without consciousness or control. Experiences do not generalize. There is no accretion of knowledge, understanding, and skills. Each situation is pristine, as though it had not happened before.

Stewart did not mean to take more than his share. He did not mean to make his mother angry. Every day he found himself in the "dog house." Somehow, he always ate for an after school snack what his mother had planned for dinner. It never occurred to Stewart that this was a possibility. All he knew was that he was hungry and the food was there. It never occurred to him to ask his mother what he might have.

Since the situation occurred over and over again the family assumed that Stewart was being defiant, and inconsiderate. They did not realize that for Stewart situations did not generalize. Each occurrence was new, as though it had not happened before.

A smile flooded Stewart's face when I told him that in the future his mother would put in a corner of the refrigerator exactly what he was free to have. He was delighted. That would "help" him. It did. This was a procedure that had to be followed in every situation until Stewart developed the capabilities necessary for behavior appropriate for family living and sharing. It was difficult for the family. They could take nothing for granted where Stewart's behavior was concerned. They had to be on constant alert for inappropriateness. Their task was made more difficult because Stewart was extremely bright. The minutia, and minutia, it was, made sense only if one understood that Stewart's brain did not come equipped with the necessary skills, and he was not acquiring them in the normal course of events. He had to be taught, much as one teaches the scales to a person who wants to play a musical instrument.

Some highly accomplished adults upon examination are found to have little more than the seedling self. They are the ones whose achievements have a marked yo-yo or teeter-totter pattern: peak experiences followed by bottom-of-the-abyss reaction. The most marked characteristic of these individuals is that their achievements bring them little more than momentary gratification. They do not experience the accretion of knowledge, understanding, and skills. The activity that has led to achievement has been automatic. They have no sense of responsibility; no consciousness of the connection between effort and accomplishment.

Had such persons not been under the direction of models (consciously or unconsciously), had they not been in a structured sequence, their activities would have been without direction, without goal. The fault is difficult to detect in these individuals, because models and structure do suffice to provide direction and goal. They substitute for the personality core. Because the fault is such a serious one, it is urgent that it be identified as early as possible and that steps be taken to correct it.

For the Parent

For the parent, the seedling or no-core self registers in:

Short attention span.
Lack of interests.
Indifference to people, things, situations.
Recklessness.
Lack of awareness of dangers and risks.

The parent must be on constant alert for mishaps due to bad judgment, inaccurate assessment of reality, and lack of concern for consequences. Parental distress is communicated in the form of anger and criticism and registers with the child the fact that he is bad, though he doesn't know why; or that there is something wrong with him, though he doesn't know what it is so he doesn't know what to do about it. Parents need to ask themselves these questions:

Does the youngster know what he did wrong?
Did he know what was wrong in it?
Did he know other ways of dealing with the situation?
What directed his choice?
Did he assess the situtation accurately?
Did he know the risks?
What can we do to help him avoid a reoccurrence of the situation?

For the Educator

For the educator the clues to the seedling, no-core self register in:

> Inability to concentrate.
> Inability to resist distraction.
> Inability to accumulate knowlege and skills.
> No sense of accomplishment.
> No satisfaction from accomplishment.
> No awareness, recognition, or respect for the interests, abilities, and rights of others.

For the Clinician

For the clinician the no-core self registers in:

> Overexpectation where others are concerned.
> Overgiving and devaluing what is given in return.
> Deferring to the wishes of others with undercurrent anger.
> Looking to others for guidelines to judgment and behavior.
> Feeling of subservience.
> No self-confidence; no trust in others, that is, no anchorage, internal or external.
> Subject to surrounding influences without judgment of events or concern for consequences.

The clinician, even though he is on the scene an infinitesimal amount of time in the individual's life, frequently finds himself the model, providing goals and direction, implicitly and explicitly. It is inevitable that he be influential in the values, priorities, and goals the individual sorts out for himself.

For the Self-Actualizer

For the self-actualizer the no-core self registers in:

> Inconsistency in performance (the peak-abyss syndrome).
> Minimum gratification from major achievement.

Disparagement of the accolades as well as the admirers.

Lack of direction or sense of purpose.

Panic at the prospect of an in-depth, long-term committed relationship.

Inability to trust self or others.

Without a firm core to self, the self-actualizer is not likely to achieve his maximum potential or derive the level of gratification justified by what he does achieve. Models and carefully structured programs can keep him on course, and his contribution to the world can be significant. The lack is qualitative and subjective. In his private life, the self-actualizer with a no-core self runs the risk of being like Henry James's Lord Mallefort, who vanished completely the moment he was alone. He had a public self but no private self with whom to be alone.

Intent on making the most of himself, the self-actualizer is likely to exceed the reach of family and friends. They are not likely to understand or appreciate his activities. The abandonment he experiences is not visible, but it is real. It is likely to be a fact of life for him unless he finds or develops what has been called a psychological family, a coterie of other self-actualizers.

The High-Level Achiever: The Self without a Core

Two patterns distinguish the high-level achiever in whose self there is no core. There is form without foundation—the donut with a hole in the middle. There are castles built on quicksand—brilliant structures that do not fulfill their promise. Some individuals find form in models and in structured situations. Others follow a dream, often hitching their wagon to another's star. Models help them select a course. External requirements of the task hold the person to it.

In both instances the individual has no sense of responsibility and experiences no sense of achievement. It is as though he had been a pawn on a chessboard with someone else determining the moves. Most significant of all is the fact that there is no conscious accretion of knowledge or skills. Such persons feel no more capable after a major achievement than before. They have been on automatic pilot. Nothing adds up to anything. Each time one program ends they face the panic of a bleak, uncharted future.

Why do these bright, talented, energetic individuals, often from loving, generous families, experience life as they do? The BONN approach suggests a number of possibilities:

> A neural network in the limbic area where the fibers are free floating, without anchorage or connections.
>
> No neural connections between the limbic section and the left hemisphere, so that realities are not communicated by the left hemisphere and therefore have no way of being registered in the brain cells of the limbic.
>
> Inadequate or nonexistent tools necessary for attention, observation, assessment, and decision making.

Experiments with laboratory animals indicate that new neural networks and neural connections can be developed through experiences. If this is true for laboratory animals, it may be assumed that it would also be true for the human being, considering the vast, unexplored potential of the human brain.

The task is two fold:

> To determine the nature of the fault.
>
> To devise procedures for correcting the fault.

The Fault: No Core/No Connections

The fault is a matter of structure: there is no center or core. There are no connections between what is experienced and what is known. Lacking these elements in structure, the self has no reality.

Rochelle was intrigued with the idea of looking in the mirror and introducing herself to herself. She had never done that. She thought it was a good idea. Being an athlete Rochelle often practiced in front of a mirror. Never had she looked into her own eyes. Actually, when she saw herself in the mirror she never really thought of the image as being herself. Now, for the first time Rochelle realized she never recognized herself in photos. That, she thought, was fascinating. She was most eager to begin the mirroring regimen. Mirroring is the very first step. It does not stand alone.

Mirroring and the Prologue

Looking at oneself face to face in the mirror gives the self form as well as substance. Individuals whose self lacks a core know they exist because they can feel their bodies. Their bodies have sensory reality but nothing else. The imprinting of form on the brain cells of the limbic area where the self has its genesis is important. It gives reality to self, a concreteness. As the self takes on this reality, it is possible that others, too, may begin to take on greater reality or concreteness. An affirmation of separateness may result from the process—a serendipity of major import in human maturation.

Mirroring may yield another bonus—increased interest in personal grooming and in creating distinctiveness in appearance. The visual reality of self is easy to achieve if the individual can address himself to it. (There are some people who find the task extremely difficult.) The psychic reality that needs to accompany mirroring is less easy. It consists of developing a statement of introduction—a "prologue to self," if you will. Each morning as the individual completes his grooming routines for the day, he stands in front of the mirror and, looking into his own eyes, presents himself: his name, whatever facts he considers important for identification, a resume of his interests, his aptitudes, his accomplishments, and finally his plans for the day. At night before he prepares for bed, he reviews before a mirror his day's accomplishments and projects his plans for the next day.

For most individuals needing to affirm, to make the self concrete, this prologue will be a self inventory. Those with no core to self will have to draw from what others have said about them, since they have no sense of their own achievement. The recitation in either case may be by rote, much as one learns the multiplication tables. The imprinting is like money in the bank. It is there to be put to use as it is needed.

A noted violinist put it well. He was urging his students to practice the scales, regularly and diligently. They weren't to concern themselves with "why." Just do it, he instructed. Don't worry about how long you will have to do the boring routines. Just do them. They may or may not take a long time. One day you will know when the routines have brought the desired results. This advice is particularly pertinent to the individual who undertakes to develop or make more firm the inner core to self.

The mirroring-prologue regimen centers. It connects and brings to an end the in-limbo, disorganized feeling that greets many individuals as they make the transition from sleep to the demands of the day.

Psychological Tools: Development

From centering and connecting, we shift to the consideration of tools. A fault of the seriousness of corelessness warrants investigation of basic equipment. A seedling self richly endowed by nature that remains a seedling self with no anchoring center signals the possibility of a flaw in the equipment required for systematic, orderly preplanned growth.

Operating on that assumption one is led to the questions: What are the tools necessary for perception of self? What are the tools necessary for processing reactions and experiences so that they add up to centering, to becoming an individual with a central organizing axis?

The processes that lead to a centered, organized self have been identified as:

Awareness: not just experiencing, but being conscious that one is experiencing and possibly even why.

Acknowledgment: recognizing that the reaction is personal, something that is real for oneself.

Assessment: Considering the significance of the reaction for oneself, perhaps for others.

Action: Making a decision as to response.

The psychological tools for achieving these processes are:

Focusing attention.
Observing.

Clustering the observations into meaningful units.

Considering the units that require action, which can range from ignoring to full involvement.

Excercises for developing these tools are simple to devise. They can be practiced in every area in which intervention is undertaken. The tools—focusing, observing, clustering, considering—are the constants. Content is the variable.

Aids to the development of a centered, organized self include:

A catalogue of feelings, beliefs, and behaviors.

Evidence of linkages or absence of linkages in the neural network.

A log of observations distinguished from feelings, beliefs, and behavior.

A catalogue of behaviors and alternative behaviors.

While the high level of self consciousness required by this regimen is short term, it is essential. It invades the visceral, sensory, and experiential pattern of reaction in the attention it gives to observations versus feelings. It increases sensitivity to and strives to sharpen the differentiation between what is observable and what is sensed without conscious awareness. The more undefined the individual's self, the more difficult the procedure will be and the longer the practice time will be necessary.

From Coreless to Firmly Centered

From coreless to firmly centered is a giant leap. It is a leap the psyche manages with ready aplomb once the requisites for spanning the gap are identified and the procedures for achieving the necessary requisities made clear. There may be initial reluctance to engage the procedures as a result of feelings of embarrassment. But the promise of a firmly centered self is inviting and intriguing. Haltingly, in these situations the procedures are brought into play. For some people the prologue is easier to implement than the mirroring. For others putting into words the activity of the moment (I am making the bed) is the beginning. A sense of excitement and achievement accompanies the effort, whatever the level at which it is undertaken. Then worries begin to surface. True, something is being gained, but what is being lost? The answer is consistent. What is about to be lost is the privilege of behavior without thought—at random, spur of the moment behavior—plus the entrenched belief in one's own infallibility. This belief has been a constant whether supported by reality or not. Replacing the random behavior would be responsibility for using knowledge and exercising logic, reason, and judgment as the realities of the situation demand. In place of infallibility would be the realization of humanness, the fact that one can be wrong. These are issues of significance. That the impact is a heady one is evidenced in the distress the psyche and the body register—a general achiness with no sign of illness, exhaustion, headaches, and inertia. And then there is the question: how different will I be? The person who has lived in tandem will wonder if he will no longer like people. The encapsulated individual will wonder if he will develop into a milquetoast and lose his individuality. The person who has lived his life in surrender and subservience will wonder whether he will lose his humanity, his concern for others.

Such worries are without foundation in knowledge, logic, reason, and judgment. They are ploys of the archaic section of the brain: the limbic section with its preference for what it knows and has had; the right hemisphere with its doom-gloom prognostications as the lure of wings (imagination) looms. The reality is that the capabilities that operated in the life-styles that served the faulty self will operate in full sway under the aegis of a full-blown self. There will be differences:

The in-tandem individual will be with people because he wants to be, not because he cannot be alone.

The encapsulated individual will continue to be a person of firm opinions, but the opinions will be based on knowledge, logic, reason, and judgement. He will have a keen sense of reality and time and not because he is aware only of his own world.

The individual who has lived in surrender will continue to give because giving brings its own reward, not because he has no other source of gratification.

The differences are qualitative. They add to pleasure and meaning for all concerned.

Reactions

The concept of a self without a core seems to gain ready response. It feels right. Often the individual experiences a hollowness. Often his sense of being is limited to body sensations; he does not seem to "be" in any firm sense. The feeling of nonbeing translates itself into a general indecisiveness: What to wear; where to go; what to do first.

The possibility that one might be able to develop a core to self so that one would not experience the internal vacuum is intriguing, even challenging; but it is accompanied invariably by caution. It feels as though it would be a difficult undertaking. The procedures prove to be simple, the process effective. Individuals find that mirroring helps them focus on themselves and what they are planning to do. It shortens markedly the time necessary to organize oneself and get going.

There comes a point where the issues are more serious. How is the individual going to use his new conscious awareness of himself and realities? Occasionally there is a person who decides he doesn't want to change the basis of his behavior. It is easier to function at random than according to knowledge, logic, reason, and judgment. He is proud of his new knowledge and awareness but decides not to put them into action.

For such individuals intervention takes an alternative route. It can focus on the development of criteria for choice of a model that the individual will seek out for goals and direction at decision-making points in his life. This is the psychological equivalent of a prosthesis, common where there are physical handicaps. The semblance of an internal core can develop in the process of following a model.

The difference between the individual with a firm internal core and one who has only the semblance of such a core is the degree of self-reliance the individual manifests. The person with a firm internal core, when he reaches maturity, sets his own standards of performance and is concerned only about the opinion of those he respects. The individual whose selfhood is externally based looks to others not only for goal setting but also for assessment of his achievements, with minimal satisfaction accruing to himself from his accomplishments.

Once there is a firm sense of self, of separateness from others, functional patterns may become more distinct.

As Roger put it, he could put himself in any one of the four patterns at one time or another. When he traveled he liked to be with someone. That would characterize him as in tandem. When Roger was with the people who meant the most to him, he insisted on having his own way, an encapsulated self. In fact, any other way seemed stupid to him, and he did not hesitate to say so. As Roger thought about that he wondered why his family and friends put up with his behavior. Of course he had no right to disparage their interests or activities. He had never been aware that was what he was doing. Carrying the analogy further, Roger could see himself in the surrendered-self category, but primarily where childern were concerned. He loved children and was particularly attracted to disabled children. He often gave up plans if they interfered with a community project on which he worked. And then there was his in-limbo self that floundered, that was without direction, without preference, a reed in the wind, subject to whatever influences happened his way. This was Roger's dominant experience, and he wanted very much to change it. He believed it was changing because Roger realized that he seemed no longer to mind being alone. As a matter of fact, he has been doing some work with wood and some painting in the hours that would traditionally have been spent at bars engaged in the sexual enterprise. Roger is beginning to have a much better feeling about himself as well as a sense of accomplishment.

There were times when Roger had the feeling of being whole. They were peak moments. They didn't hold. Roger was continuing the mirroring technique along with the soliloqy. He was beginning to be more aware of and concerned about other people's reactions to him—how he looked, what he said. Sexual compulsion had disappeared, and he was feeling much better physically. Most of all his job performance had improved markedly, and he was receiving public recognition, which he was enjoying to the fullest. Roger wanted very much to become a fully autonomous, authentic self. He was well on the way.

An Alert

One must be aware that venturing to invade the self, to examine its level of functioning and consider whether it has the necessary psychic tools, represents a major assault on the psyche. Sensitivity on the part of the intervener is of paramount importance. Resistances must be recognized and respected. Withdrawals must be appreciated and accepted as the individual's right. Organic reactions (headaches and general achiness with no other symptoms of illness) must be considered as possible indicators that internal stress is overreaching the individual's tolerance.

The Self: Intervention Preparation

Invasion of self, especially the structural aspects of self, may be undertaken only if the individual:

Is fully aware of the condition that will be under examination.

Understands the reason why this is being considered: the potential gains, the possible risks—what the individual may have to give up.

Realizes that there will be specific procedures to be followed without understanding the "why" of them.

Understands that there may be reactions: physical—fatigue, ravenous hunger; psychological—a self-consciousness, insecurity, a feeling of not knowing what to do next in familiar situations, much like the centipede, who

Never had any trouble running
Until the toad in fun
Asked him which foot came after which
Whereupon he lay immobilized in the ditch.

The centipede's experience is graphic and familiar. There are those who having experienced it want none of it. They prefer not knowing. They prefer behaving on the impulse of the moment and trusting what they do will be OK. Their preference must be honored and the course of action altered accordingly.

Self/Other

In the self-other context personality characteristics come into play. They will be examined from two vantage points: sectional centrality and the three basic laws of nature.

Personality Characteristics: Sectional Centrality

The Limbic Personality

The individual in whom the limbic section is dominant is easy to identify. He is people-focused, more concerned about having friends than developing his own interests and talents. Being liked is of primary importance even though to achieve popularity he must forego his own preferences. He tends to give too much and suffer in silence the intensity of the hurt he feels when his giving is not reciprocated. As a child a limbic personality would rather play than study; is more concerned about a football score than a school grade. As an adult his expectations of others are likely to be excessive and without consideration of the other individual's reality. Mrs. T. is a case in point.

> Mrs. T. lives life in anger and frustration, with a pervasive sense of abandonment and a feeling of being totally unloved and unimportant. Her only son spends little time with her, and is rarely available to help her with chores or even in emergencies. She knows he is deeply involved in the management of a very complex, important scientific enterprise. She knows that his wife and three adolescent children require much of the little free time he has. She knows by the way he looks that he is harrassed, straining his physical and emotional resources much beyond what is wise or healthy. She often worries that he, like his father, will not live long enough to retire. Her perceptions of his reality are accurate. They do not stem her feelings of abandonment, of being unloved. Her anger disconnects the left hemisphere and the limbic area as it often does, rendering knowledge, logic, and reason inoperable.

The Right Hemisphere Personality

The individual dominated by the right hemisphere is the dreamer.

Don wanted to be a scientist but he couldn't tolerate math, chemistry, or physics.

Dot wanted to be an interesting conversationalist but she didn't like to read.

Todd wanted to be a millionaire by the age of forty but he couldn't keep a job for more than six months. When he worked his earnings were squandered at the race track.

Each of these individuals had dreams. They wanted what they wanted. They functioned as though wishing would make it so. Right hemisphere fantasy was in control. Unless left hemisphere knowledge, logic, reason, and judgment were brought into play and achieved control their dreams would never be realized.

The Left Hemisphere Personality

The individual whose left hemisphere dominates is firmly rooted in reality. He has no illusions about magic or magical power. He learns early and quickly that things do not just happen. One must make them happen. The questions "why?" and "how do you know?" plague him and those who share his world. Sometimes the "we don't know" spurs investigation. Sometimes it ignites futility. How fortunate such individuals are if among their nurturers and mentors there are those who view knowledge and life as emergent. I was one such fortunate person.

I was in my mid-thirties. I had been in my profession twelve years but was beginning a new job in a new field. My mind was exploding with questions. The executive who had undertaken to initiate me listened patiently, impassionately. Finally, a simple response: "Those are questions you are here to help us answer." No one in all of my eighteen years of school experience had ever suggested that all questions did not have answers. If they did, I didn't hear it. That simple response held a double message for me: not only were all the answers not in, not all the questions had even been asked. And my life was turned around. It was at that moment that I as a searcher, a researcher, was born.

The left hemisphere-dominated individual is likely to be short on emotions and imagination. He is likely to prefer his own company to the company of others. He is likely to engage in social activities to meet expectations rather than in response to his own needs.

The Mixed-Dominance Personality

In some individuals sectional dominance is shared. Most often the sharing involves the limbic section and the right hemisphere. Occasionally the dominance is shared three ways. These individuals describe their brain function as chaotic, and truly it is. The shared dominance can follow a cyclical pattern or it can be random, triggered by unidentifiable stimuli.

The individual in whom sectional dominance is shared is an enigma to himself and to all who know him. He is likely to be bright, talented, energetic, and adventuresome. The promise he presents is multidimensional, lavish. Whatever he undertakes to do, his initial efforts are superlative. He is like a blazing comet that streaks across the sky—brilliant but passing. There is no sustaining power or any accretion of skill. The individual has achieved no expertise. Concentration, commitment, and dedication are difficult. His desire to become a scientist is thwarted by his right hemisphere fantasy that all he needs to know or know how to do exists in his brain cells. What he needs to do is unearth what he knows. His desire to become a musician is thwarted by his overwhelming intrigue with the orchestrations in his mind (right hemisphere). His wish to be married and have children is thwarted by his preoccupation with his many varied interests. He has little to give or share in relationships.

Disorders

Where disorders are concerned we may expect depression in the limbic personality; schizophrenia in the right hemisphere personality; detachment and depersonalization in the left hemisphere personality; and manic depression in the mixed-dominance personality.

Personality Characteristics:
The Basic Laws of Nature

If one examines personality characteristics in terms of the three basic laws of nature interesting patterns come to light:

> There are individuals who want to do nothing more than eat, sleep, and enjoy sex. They do not consider any task beneath their dignity. They enjoy routine. They do not require challenge or variety (the law of gravity or inertia).
>
> In dramatic contrast is the individual for whom routine is anathema, intolerable for any length of time. These people need variety, challenge, and adventure (the law of magnetism). Often individuals subject to the law of inertia are drawn to those subject to the law of magnetism. The intrigue is short-lived for the law of inertia is strong, and developing the attributes that go with the law of magnetism is difficult. It can be done but firm commitment and great patience are required.
>
> Other individuals are subject to the law of conservation. History is their love. Antiques proved a magnetic fascination (the law of conservation).

An urgent question finds voice when one relates personality characteristics to the laws of nature: Does that mean we can't change? A dramatic answer is found in our technological achievements. We conquered the law of gravity in order to reach the moon. There is no doubt, given the vast potential for change in the human brain, that feats of equal magnitude can be achieved where the human personality is concerned. We need to understand the phenomenon with which we are dealing. We need to develop the techniques for accomplishing the task. Effort, energy, and firm determination are certain to be essential.

Intervention

Difficulties in the self/other dimension (relationships) stem primarily from the issue of separateness, one of the absolutes of life experience. Everyone is separate and distinct and once fully developed is designed by nature to function as an independent, autonomous organism.

The womb experience is deeply imprinted in the limbic section brain cells. The psychological umbilical cord instead of self-destructing as does the physical umbilical cord is nurtured in twentieth-century, Western culture by such songs as "You're nobody, till somebody loves you"; "Love is all there is . . . love will see you through"; "People who need people are the luckiest people in the world." This is fantasy, fantasy of the first order.

In a mobile society where your best friends are likely to be strangers on the move, you had better be somebody if you want somebody even to acknowledge you are around, let alone love you. Love at best is illusive. It defies definition. We are in the process of accumulating massive evidence that love cannot be mandated. It comes with no guarantee or warranty. It is a high-risk enterprise not only because of its volatility but because of its toll when failure strikes.

Mobility is only one of the conditions that complicates the self/other task. Another of at least equal significance is our ever-rising expectations. As one young woman put it: "Things are OK. I want them to be great."

It was 1970. I was speaking to a group of young professionals ranging in age from twenty-four to thirty. The subject was "The Premarital Household." Their main concern was that their parents didn't understand. My concern was that I wasn't sure they "understood." They certainly weren't happy with my point of view—that is, each person had to determine what was right for him. Hopefully, the choice would reflect values, priorities, and goals. They felt I had "copped out." I felt they were not addressing some basic issues. The issue was joined when I asked: "If you took comfort, convenience, security, and sex out of marriage, what would you have?" There was a long silence. Finally, a man way in the back ventured sheepishly: "Maybe we should be selecting our dates from interest groups." It was as though this had never before occurred to him. A woman, in response, asserted with hostility: "That would be nice."

The group rejected the possibility that human beings might be like mountain goats—interested in the opposite sex only at mating time. The women particularly believed that men and women had something to contribute to each other that would enrich life. Neither the men nor the women were clear as to what that "something" was, beyond gender. They soberly conceded that something was amiss and missing in the man-woman relationship as it was being experienced currently and that unless this was corrected we might indeed witness the demise of marriage as a social institution.

Where the self/other is concerned the psychological dimension must be addressed, especially in our Western world. We must pay attention to sectional centrality and to the three basic laws of nature as they are reflected in personality and behavior. Perhaps as our knowledge in these areas increases we will be able to develop guidelines for selecting the people in our lives that will be more effective than astrology and the computer.

Self/Situation

Self and self/other are limbic issues. Situation takes us into the domain of the left hemisphere. Situation is definable, specific, and objective. It brings into play options, alternatives, and realities, external and internal.

Peg was distraught. Thoughts of suicide kept invading her days and nights. She was frightened. She had just completed an advanced degree in her favorite subject, anthropology. She had an excellent job and was slated for promotion. She had a great deal to live for. Peg had worked hard to achieve what she had.

She was pretty sure it was her marriage that was giving her trouble. And even that didn't make sense. She and her husband had wonderful times together on vacation and on weekends. They enjoyed the same things. What was wrong was subtle, yet pervasive. Peg wondered if she was losing her mind. She didn't think so. But she couldn't be sure.

Eight years ago, when Peg and Lem married Peg couldn't imagine that Lem really meant it when he said "no children." His first family of four sons, now young adults, were enough. Peg had imagined that his children might substitute for her children. Little did she expect their hostility. They were irreconcilable where she was concerned. She could do nothing right. It apparently never occurred to them that their father's continuing generosity with them was something she shared in and was deprived by. Of course, she would never tell them. But her anger was mounting. Not only could she not have the children she longed for, but her dream house seemed farther away with each passing year. It would probably never be. Peg was beginning to wonder what there was in this marriage for her.

Peg was young. It was her youth and the fantasies of the May to December romance that indulged her dream of four adolescents becoming her children by proxy. It was her inexperience, and her wishing-would-make-it-so idea that led her to set aside concern for Lem and what his first family meant to him. She was wanting to wipe clean the slate of Lem's pre-Peg life. It couldn't be done.

Peg would need to make her peace with the fact that there had been a part of Lem's life in which she had had no part and in which she probably could have no share, not necessarily because Lem did not want it; rather because others did not want it. Another reality even more difficult to accept was the fact that only Lem could decide what portion of his resources were to go to his first family and how much to his second. Peg's only recourse was to decide whether what he was willing to share with her was enough. Rights. Prerogatives. Options. These were the issues to be examined against the backdrop of the values, priorities, and goals of each participant.

Basic to the consideration of rights, prerogatives, and options are some absolutes:

Everyone as far as we know has only one life to live.

In the United States each individual is believed to have the right to life, liberty, and the pursuit of happiness.

My freedom ends with your nose.

Two people do not and cannot make one. Each is separate and distinct, with his own predesigned personality, his own genetic history, and his own life experience. Difference is nature's trademark. It should carry with it the promise of enrichment, of expansion.

Summary

This chapter has focused on techniques for developing selfhood, separateness, and the building blocks for situation management. The presenting problem is where we begin. The "why" problem is addressed only to determine the nature of the problem and the section of the brain in which its roots may be lodged. Commitment to change and to left hemisphere control of brain functioning are the only requisites. Techniques are selected on the basis of the nature of the fault to be addressed: the structure of self; sectional centrality; the laws of nature. The major task is to equip the left hemisphere with the knowledge it needs to be in control of brain functioning and to be sure there are the necessary neural channels to carry left hemisphere mandates to the limbic section and the right hemisphere. Left hemisphere development includes the accretion of knowledge and the development of the skill necessary for the exercise of logic, reason, and judgment.

CHAPTER 7

Summation

The BONN approach to personality and behavior draws from brain research for information on brain organization and design. It draws from the natural sciences commitment to the belief in the vast untapped potential in the human organism.

Translating brain research findings into therapeutic techniques has been a heady experience. Like the hunter who tracks a rabbit and traps a bear, the intellectual explorer far outreaches the bounds of his imagination. New insights continue to surface. Sometimes the view is microscopic; sometimes, telescopic. The familiar "the world in a grain of sand" takes on new meaning. The scientists' view of an ever-expanding universe is affirmed.

Results

The results that stand out as most significant are:

The BONN approach puts the individual in command of the operation of the three sections of the brain. With a few simple procedures one can keep mind wandering, daydreaming, and the doom-disaster syndrome under control. With a few simple procedures one can keep limbic impulsiveness in tow and upgrade the level of limbic functioning.

The BONN approach provides the rationale and the program for developing left hemisphere knowledge and skills so that the left hemisphere can assume and maintain control over the archaic sections. Attendant on the development of left hemisphere knowledge and skills is the development of neural channels for knowledge and skill transmission to the archaic sections. Practice is the essential tool to neural channel development.

The BONN approach has been dramatically effective in dealing with learning difficulties, marital stress, sexual compulsion, and marginal and blatant psychoses.

There are indications that the BONN approach can bring smoking and obesity under control. There are also sufficient signs that it may be effective with individuals of criminal bent to warrant exploration and experimentation.

The BONN approach has revealed faults in the structure and function of the self that seriously affect the operation of the executive "I." It has devised procedures for correcting these faults.

The BONN approach is liberating. It frees individuals and their nurturers and mentors of responsibililty. Whatever the faults, they are faults in the organization or design of the brain as preset by nature. There may be faults too in such psychological tools as perception, observation, and assessment. Correction in each of these areas is possible through the use of simple procedures systematically practiced.

Conclusion

The BONN approach holds great promise for individuals of all ages irrespective of their prior life experience, provided there is at least a marginal awareness of reality and provided there is the wish to change.

A new life begins the moment one decides to wrest authority from instinct, reflex, and habit and engages the powerful forces of knowledge, logic, reason, and judgment that are firmly rooted in reality and time.

Appendix

Concepts presented in Dr. Margaret Golton's Theory of BONN. Prepared by Bonita Vargo, doctoral student, Cornell University, November 1982.

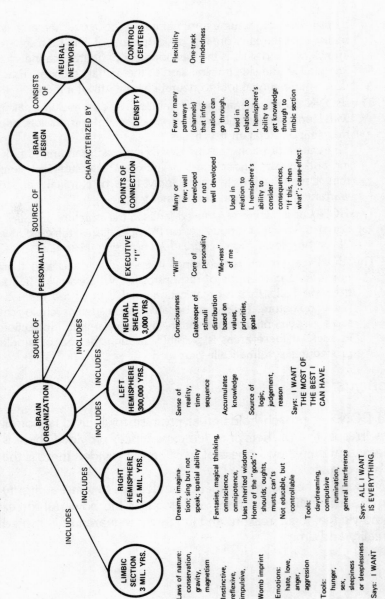

BRAIN ORGANIZATION — SOURCE OF — **PERSONALITY** — SOURCE OF — **BRAIN DESIGN** — CONSISTS OF — **NEURAL NETWORK**

INCLUDES: **LIMBIC SECTION 3 MIL. YRS.**, **RIGHT HEMISPHERE 2.5 MIL. YRS.**, **LEFT HEMISPHERE 300,000 YRS.**, **NEURAL SHEATH 3,000 YRS**

INCLUDES (Personality): **EXECUTIVE "I"**

CHARACTERIZED BY: **POINTS OF CONNECTION**, **DENSITY**, **CONTROL CENTERS**

LIMBIC SECTION 3 MIL. YRS.

Laws of nature: conservation, gravity, magnetism

Instinctive, reflexive, impulsive,

Womb imprint

Emotions: hate, love, anger, aggression

Tools: hunger, sex, sleepiness or sleeplessness

Says: I WANT

RIGHT HEMISPHERE 2.5 MIL. YRS.

Dreams, imagination; sing but not speak; spatial ability

Fantasies, magical thinking, omniscience, omnipotence,

Uses inherited wisdom

Home of the "gods"; shoulds, oughts, musts, can'ts

Not educable, but controllable

Tools: daydreaming, compulsive rumination, general interference

Says: ALL I WANT IS EVERYTHING.

LEFT HEMISPHERE 300,000 YRS.

Sense of reality, time sequence

Accumulates knowledge

Source of logic, judgement, reason

Says: I WANT THE MOST OF THE BEST I CAN HAVE.

NEURAL SHEATH 3,000 YRS

Consciousness

Gatekeeper of stimuli distribution based on values, priorities, goals

EXECUTIVE "I"

"Will"

Core of personality

"Me-ness" of me

POINTS OF CONNECTION

Many or few; well developed or not well developed

Used in relation to l. hemisphere's ability to consider consequences, "If this, then what"; cause-effect

DENSITY

Few or many pathways (channels) that information can go through.

Used in relation to l. hemisphere's ability to get knowledge through to limbic section

CONTROL CENTERS

Flexibility

One-track mindedness

THE IDEA BEHIND CHANGING PERSONALITY LIES IN DECISION AND COMMITMENT TO PRACTICE NEW BEHAVIORS, TO DEVELOP NEW NEURAL CHANNELS/CONNECTIONS OR ATROPHY PREVIOUSLY USED ONES. DIFFICULTY SPRINGS FROM TENDENCY TOWARD INERTIA AND SENIORITY AND POWER OF ARCHAIC SYSTEMS.

RECOGNIZES UNIQUENESS OF EACH BRAIN DESIGN PRESET AT BIRTH AND ITS REDESIGN; SEES MALADJUSTMENT NOT IN TERMS OF PATHOLOGY BUT TYPE OF BRAIN DESIGN AND ADEQUACY OF SAME.

Notes

1. Claire Rayner, *Mind and Body* (New York: Rand McNally, 1976), p. 80.
2. Colin Blakemore, *Mechanics of the Mind* (London: Cambridge University Press, 1976), p. 45.
3. Lael Wertenbaker, *The Eye: Window to the World* (Washington, D.C.: U.S. News Books, 1981), pp. 51 and 56.
4. Wertenbaker, p. 49.

BIBLIOGRAPHY

Brown, Barbara. *Supermind.* New York: Harper & Row, 1980.

Cassidy, Harold G. *Science Restated.* San Francisco: Freeman Cooper, 1970.

Corbellis, Michael, and Beale, Ivan. *The Psychology of Left and Right.* Hillsdale N.Y.: Lawrence Erlbaum, 1976.

Forsee, Alyesa. *Beneath Land and Sea.* Philadelphia: McCral Smith, 1962.

Fuller, Buckminster. *Ideas and Integrities.* Englewood Cliffs, N.J.: Prentice-Hall, 1969.

Furst, Charles. *Origins of the Mind–Brain Connection.* Englewood Cliffs, N.J.: Prentice-Hall, 1979.

Gardner, John W. *Self-Renewal.* New York: Harper & Row, 1965.

Gruber, Howard, and Barrett, Paul. *Darwin on Man.* New York: Dutton, 1974.

Guillemien, Victor. *The Story of Quantum Mechanics.* New York: Scribners, 1968.

Heisenberg, Werner. *Across the Frontiers.* New York: Harper & Row, 1974.

Janov, Arthur. *Primal Man: The New Consciousness.* New York: Crowell, 1975.

Judson, Horace F. *The Search for Solutions.* New York: Holt, Rinehart and Winston, 1980.

Kestenbaum, Robert, and Aisenberg, Ruth. *The Psychology of Death.* New York: Springer, 1972.

LeComte, Du Nouy. *Human Destiny.* New York: Mentor Books, 1947.

Levinson, Daniel J. *The Seasons of a Man's Life.* New York: Knopf, 1978.

Lygne, David G. *Life Manipulation.* New York: Walker, 1970.

Nourse, Elan E. *Universe, Earth and Atom.* New York: Harper & Row, 1969.

Ogburn, Charlton. *The Adventure of Birds.* New York: Morrow, 1976.

Panati, Charles. *Breakthroughs.* Boston: Houghton Mifflin, 1980.

Pelletier, Kenneth R. *Towards a Science of Consciousness.* New York: Dell, 1978.

Pfeiffer, John E. *The Emergence of Man.* New York: Harper & Row, 1969.

Pribram, Karl. "Holographic Memory," *Psychology Today.* Vol. 12, Feb. 1979, pp. 72–84.

Restak, Richard M. *The Brain: The Last Frontier.* New York: Doubleday, 1979.

Reusch, Bernard. *Homosapiens.* New York: Columbia University Press, 1972.

Rifkin, Jeremy. *Entrophy.* New York: Viking, 1980.

Rose, Steven. *The Conscious Brain.* New York: Knopf, 1973.

Rosenfeld, Albert, ed. *Mind and Supermind.* New York: Holt, Rinehart and Winston, 1977.

Russell, Peter. *The Brain Book.* New York: Hawthorne Books, 1979.

Schrag, Peter. *Mind Control.* New York: Pantheon, 1978.

Silverstein, Alvin. *The Conquest of Death.* New York: Macmillan, 1979.

Snyder, Paul. *Health and Human Nature.* Ontario, Canada, Chilton Book Company, 1980.

Springer, Deutsch. *Left Brain, Right Brain.* San Francisco: Freeman, 1981.

Thomas, Lewis. *The Medusa and the Snail.* New York: Viking, 1979.

Toffler, Alvin. *Future Shock.* New York: Random House, 1970.

Trefil, James. *From Atoms To Quarks.* New York: Scribner's, 1980.

Whimbey, Arthur. *Intelligence Can Be Taught.* New York: Dutton, 1975.

Wilson, Colin. *Starseekers.* New York: Doubleday, 1980.

Wolman, Benjamin B., ed. *International Encyclopedia of Psychiatry, Psychology, and Neurology.* New York: Aesculepius Publications, 1977.

Young, J. Z. *Programs of the Brain.* Oxford, England, Oxford University Press, 1978.